# 15 Minute FAMILY TRADITIONS & MEMORIES

*Emilie Barnes*

**HARVEST HOUSE PUBLISHERS**
Eugene, Oregon 97402

**15-Minute Family Traditions and Memories**
Copyright ©1995 by Harvest House Publishers
Eugene, Oregon 97402

Library of Congress Cataloging-in-Publication Data

Barnes, Emilie.
    15 minute family traditions & memories / Emilie Barnes.
        p. cm.
    ISBN 1-56507-371-1
    1. Family festivals—United States.  2. Family—United States—Religious life.
3. Holidays—United States.  4. United States—Social life and customs.  I. Title
GT2402.U6B37    1995                                          95-13303
394.2–dc20                                                          CIP
                                                                    AC

95 96 97 98 99 00 01 — 10 9 8 7 6 5 4 3 2 1

# Dedication

To my Bob, who has encouraged me to be the woman God wants me to be. He has helped me to use my creativity in making our home a warm and happy place to live. We have made some beautiful memories and started warm traditions together which we have passed down to our children and grandchildren.

Being raised in a Jewish home, I had many traditions, but it wasn't until my Bob led me to the Messiah that our real holiday traditions were created, thus making this book possible. I am grateful for my Jewish heritage which is now complete in Christ, who brings joy to our hearts and homes.

# Contents

# Measure Your Moments...
## Treasure Your Memories

As we live in this hectic world that says, "Faster, faster, you must go faster," our souls cry out, "Slower, slower, I must go slower." What a conflict between what we hear and what we want to do!

In Romans 12:2 (NIV) Paul writes, "Do not conform any longer to the pattern of this world, but be transformed by the renewing of your mind. Then you will be able to test and approve what God's will is—his good, pleasing and perfect will."

When we take time in our hurried lives to create memories through the things we do, we are in essence saying, "Lord, what is important for me and my family's life? Show me what is important for everyday living. How can I beat the system?"

There was no Christmas, no tree, no parties, no gifts, no cookie exchange, no ornaments hung or given, no excitement, no wish list—just one little girl looking out a window, longing to be involved in the most beautiful season of the year.

I was raised in a Jewish home. Yes, there was love, there was food, and there was Hanukkah. I was different, but I wanted to be like everyone else—enjoying Christmas carols, Christmas shopping, Santa, sleigh bells, reindeer and, most of all, Christmas traditions.

I was 11 when my father died. My mother became even stronger in the Jewish faith, and I went weekly to Hebrew school and temple. It wasn't kosher to celebrate Christmas. God, however, had other plans for me. God brought a young man into my life who did celebrate Christmas, did believe in Jesus as Messiah, and did participate in all the beautiful traditions of the Christmas holiday. My heart was touched by Christ's love as Bob shared the true Christmas story with me one evening: that God did have a Son, His name is Jesus, and He is the Messiah our people are waiting for. Bob shared how Jesus said, "I am the way, and the truth, and the life; no one comes to the Father but through Me" (John 14:6), and "I came that they might have life, and might have it abundantly" (John 10:10).

Bob's Christian heritage and upbringing surfaced strongly during those early dating months and, through his loving influence, I received Christ into my heart and became a believing Christian. We were married a year later, and I'll never forget our first Christmas together—for me the very first Christmas of my life. Money was short, but we had a tree and gave each other ornaments, which became a tradition for our family.

Holidays are wonderful opportunities to develop lasting memories built around family traditions. Traditions are similar to habits. They may be either detrimental or beneficial. We need to understand why certain traditions are observed, the messages that they convey, and how they affect our lives.

In Proverbs 24:3,4 (NIV) we read, "By wisdom a house is built, and through understanding it is established; through knowledge its rooms are filled with rare and beautiful treasures." The writer encourages us to use wisdom, understanding, and knowledge to create homes filled with rare and beautiful treasures. These words of encouragement certainly put us into action.

This book, *15-Minute Family Traditions and Memories*, is written to help you, the reader, to measure your moments and treasure your memories. Creating family traditions isn't done in a vacuum, but through activities year-round. Be an observer of life. Seek ways to teach on a variety of occasions. In Deuteronomy 6:7, Moses instructs the people when he says, "You shall teach them diligently to your sons and shall talk of them when you sit in your house and when you walk by the way and when you lie down and when you rise up."

We are to live life with a godly purpose. For many years I thought I was raising children for the moment, not realizing that I was teaching for generations to come. The things I taught my children are now being taught by them to my grandchildren. Time flees from us so quickly. We pause for a moment, take several deep breaths, and find ourselves to be grandparents and great-grandparents.

Use this book to give you wisdom, understanding, and knowledge in raising those children so they can truly say, "I treasure my memories. The traditions that I learned and lived with while growing up have made me the person who I am today."

# 1

*Learn to Create*
*Treasured Memories*

IN OUR HECTIC EFFORTS to make a living and meet all the demands upon our 24 hours per day, we are often too exhausted to spend quality time together as a family to create treasured memories. When a slower day comes, we just want to lay back and do nothing. It becomes a catch-up day so we can be ready to start again. We continually ask, "How do I get off this treadmill?" We have to do it on purpose. Learn to create treasured memories! They don't happen by chance. For the family to endure today, we have to plan for success. Let's take time to live life with a purpose.

I want to give special encouragement to Mom and Dad to work as a team to make life meaningful. Children love to see their parents working with a plan. If Dad is reluctant to get involved, then Mom will have to carry the extra load to live life with a purpose. Planning ahead for memories will also give single parents an extra spurt of energy for living life with a quality of memories.

You don't need money to create memories; you just need a desire. As adults, many of our memories are from our childhood or from when we were first married. Looking back to our early married life, Bob and I had very little money, but we have many fond memories. Now we have much more financial independence, but our early memories are still very vivid. Someone shared with me once, "Successful people do what unsuccessful people aren't willing to do." That statement had a real impact on my life. From that day on, I began to identify what those things were. One that was brought to mind was that successful people planned their lives. I wasn't planning my life very well at the time. Since then, I have learned to create treasured memories.

A memory-builder doesn't have to be limited to one season of the year or a certain holiday. It can be any event that later becomes a happy memory—a family ritual, a season, a tradition, or even the creation of a memorable event out of an ordinary day. A memory-builder might be:

- Having a "Bowl Game Party" each New Year's Day.

- Thanksgiving Day at Grandma's house with her favorite turkey recipe.

- Trout fishing the last two weeks of August in Idaho.

- A tea party with Grammy in the garden.

- Ice fishing on the lake each December with Uncle Bill.

- Boiling and coloring eggs for Easter baskets.

- Going to the beach for the Fourth of July and roasting hot dogs and watching a fireworks display.

- Telephoning a family member each year on his or her birthday at the exact time the person was born.

- Flying a special birthday flag by the front door when someone in the family has a birthday.

- Eating off a special plate for that special occasion.

- Having Dad read the Christmas story in the Gospel of Luke before the main meal on Christmas Day.

- Having Mom place lit candles on the table at dinnertime.

- Spending a week at a lake in a cabin each summer.

- Swimming in the ocean each January along with the rest of the members of the local Polar Bear Club.

+ Going to Mexico each summer on the church's work trip to help missionaries.

+ Helping feed the homeless in the city on Thanksgiving Day.

## Develop Family Traditions

I often question ladies who attend my seminars about traditions they had in their families while growing up—traditions that set them apart as belonging to that unique family (a sign, a thumbs-up, a kiss on the nose, a pinch of the cheek). I found that most people had no such traditions. Some even asked, "What's a tradition?" or said "We had no traditions at all, even at Christmastime, birthdays, or anniversaries."

From reading my books, you know very well that I am a strong believer in family traditions. I have found that it takes only a small gesture to bring families closer. Traditions help you connect with your family and maintain those ties.

Many of these traditions have been used by our own family or are ones that have been shared by many of the ladies who attend my seminars or read my books. There are more ideas than you can use. Select a few that interest you and try them on your family members. My Bob tells me that you are never too old to start a new tradition. So let's start now. . . .

### ∞ *A Butterfly Kiss*

My Bob gives the grandchildren a "butterfly kiss" by fluttering his eyelashes on the children's cheeks. They just love it. Another one (which I won't describe) is a "car-wash kiss." You can guess what that's like.

### ∞ *A special handshake*

My Bob greets a certain male friend and his two grown sons

with a special greeting. They shake hands, slip down to a clasp of the fingertips, quickly move into a thumb grip, shift to a knock on the elbow, and finish with a big smile. Only men will probably want to do that—it's not very dainty for women.

## ∞ Silent Communication

Invent a silent symbol of your family's camaraderie. For example, a thumbs-up, a wink, or a tug on the earlobe.

## ∞ Kid Fix

Request a "kid fix"—a hefty hug and a big kiss—whenever you feel the need. Let your youngsters know it makes you feel much better.

## ∞ Once a Day

Tell your children you love them at least once every 24 hours—when you send them off to school, when they come home, when you pray with them at night, or anytime.

## ∞ Go Ahead, Try It

Encourage your child to try new things: taste unusual foods, enter contests, write for information on subjects that interest him or her.

## ∞ Double Desserts

Once a month, surprise your family by announcing double-dessert night.

## ∞ Yogurt Run

During the summer or when the children don't have school

the next day, go into their rooms just before they fall asleep and announce a "yogurt run." They will think you have flipped out, but they will always remember the special times when you got them out of bed and went to get some delightful yogurt.

### ∞ You Are Special Today

We have a large red plate which has inscribed on it: "You Are Special Today." We are always honoring a member of the family or guest who comes to dinner. We've even taken this plate to restaurants, on a picnic, and to a beach party. We let the special person use that special plate. We also take a photograph of that person and place the picture in a special photo album that houses pictures of our recipients.

### ∞ Sharing a Secret

You can have a lot of fun by sharing a secret and keeping up the suspense until Christmas or a birthday comes. It's also good training to teach the children how to keep a secret.

### ∞ What's the Best Thing That Happened to You Today?

Quite often we ask this question toward the end of our meal, and the discussion that follows keeps the family for a longer time at the table and keeps us talking. No TV is allowed during dinner.

### ∞ Mom's Canned Questions

We have a jar of 150 questions that are great for the family to answer in a constructive way during any mealtime. Many times we even use this jar of questions when our adult friends come to visit.

### ∞ Cooking Class

At least once a month set aside a special afternoon where the children are invited to the kitchen to prepare a meal or a portion of a meal. Desserts are always a winner. Bring out the aprons and chef's hat. If they dress like cooks, they will really get involved in the process.

### ∞ Bravo!

Three cheers for success! Honor a child who does well in an activity, on a test, a term report, or by completing a chore. Make it a big deal—you might even cook the person's favorite meal.

### ∞ Young Decorator

When sprucing up your children's rooms, allow them to pick the color theme, paint, sheets, curtains, or towels. If that's too risky, give them specific choices (several wallpaper designs, three or four paints, or choices of several bedspreads).

### ∞ Study Hall

Select that special area at home (a table, a couch, a chair) to review materials to be covered in a test tomorrow. Have your children cozy up and get comfortable in their special "study hall."

### ∞ What a Fine Family We Have

I'm one for framing family pictures all over the house: individuals and group pictures from last summer's vacation, a winter ski trip, or a Christmas group picture. Be sure to share these pictures in the children's rooms, too. This gives them a great sense of family identity.

### ∞ Cowbell

I have an old cowbell that is positioned by our kitchen door. Two minutes before a meal is to be served, I go out and ring that bell very firmly. This is a signal to the members of the family that the food is ready. They have two minutes to get to the table.

## ∞ *How Pretty*

Let your children wear your old jewelry and dress up when they have playtime.

## ∞ *Sorry*

Admit when you're wrong. Your family members know when you've blown it as well as you do.

## ∞ *Pet Names*

As the children get older, don't drop those pet names, but use them privately to avoid embarrassing the kids.

## ∞ *Those School Projects*

Use those special clay vases that are brought home as flower vases or to hold paper clips.

## ∞ *I'm Like Dad*

Lend your son a tie to wear on special occasions.

## ∞ *I Choose You*

Tell your children how much you enjoy being their parents. Kids like to hear they are loved.

## ∞ *A Warm Bear Hug*

There's nothing like going to bed on a cold night with a warm teddy bear at your side. Sew flannel, fake fur, or other cuddly material into a teddy bear that will fit around a hot-water-bottle. You can use a zipper in the back to close the seam. A button or a safety pin also works nicely. Stuff the arms, legs, and head with polyester fiberfill, rags, or old nylons.

As the child is getting ready for bed, fill the bottle with hot water and tuck the bear between the sheets. Your child will look forward to going to bed.

## ∽ Flannel Sheets in the Winter

For our grandchildren's birthdays, I give them a package of designer flannel sheets and pillowcases. Their mom puts them on the beds when the weather turns cold. They just love these warm, soft sheets that make getting into bed so inviting. It also brings back fond memories of their birthday parties.

## ∽ Worship Services at Home

There are many times during the year when you might not be able to attend your regular church due to inclement weather, sickness, or being away on a vacation.

Plan your own worship service with the children. Sing familiar hymns and choruses using any instruments that the family can play. One of the children might even like to lead your group in song. Go around the group and share prayer requests. This is a great opportunity to be transparent and reveal where hurts and needs are in the family unit. The children might like to mention friends at school who need prayer. Share blessings from the week. Give an opportunity for prayer. Let the children feel free to pray however they wish. This is a great time to model praying out loud. Our grandchildren love to give devotions on some passage from a previous Sunday school lesson. Dad can always be ready to share from a section of Scripture that he has been studying. In closing, make sure that everyone gets a warm hug with an "I love you."

## ∞ Family Night

Designate one night a week as family night. Rotate among the family members who will choose the activity for that evening. It might be ice-skating, bowling, roller-skating, frying hamburgers, going to the beach to swim, going out to dinner, etc. These can be very special times when people in a family get to know each other better. Our children always enjoyed family nights because they were so much fun.

## ∞ Pennies at the Bottom of the Sink

I was able to get our children—and now our grandchildren— to wash the evening dishes by occasionally dropping some pennies into the bottom of the sudsy water. The kids were always thrilled to find these copper treasures.

## ∞ Grandpa's Treasures

Grandpas have special privileges, and one of them is to make sure that the grandchildren always know that Grandpa has a secret treasure in his shirt pocket. It might be chewing gum, candy, a certificate for something—even some loose change. On occasion, my Bob takes his loose change out of his pocket and divides it among the grandchildren. They like to be around Grandpa because he's so much fun.

## ∞ Go to the Fun Box

Somewhere near the dining room table have a fun box that contains slips of paper listing activities for the family. The box can be plain, or it can be creatively decorated with bright paper or paint. Make sure that the box has a lid, but make an opening that allows room for a small hand to reach inside.

On slips of paper, the family can write down various activities:

- ✦ Renting a video
- ✦ Going bowling
- ✦ Going to the movies
- ✦ Reading a favorite book together
- ✦ Going for a walk
- ✦ Singing favorite songs
- ✦ Making cookies
- ✦ Popping popcorn

When things drag around the home and you need to pump a little life into the day, have a family member go over to the box and draw out a slip of paper. Whatever is on that paper becomes the evening's activity. Make sure that only fun ideas are inserted into the box. Once an idea is used, it can be put back into the box if everyone enjoyed the activity. If not, drop in an idea for a new activity for a future draw.

## Creating Special Occasions

As a child growing up, I didn't have a lot of fond memories. Our family had more dysfunction than function. However, I do remember my father taking me to a pier and dropping a fishing line over the side. I don't remember us catching any fish, but Dad and I had some precious times together. One of my fondest memories was created when we celebrated the Festival of Lights at Hanukkah time. My Uncle Hy and Uncle Saul would play the violin and piano, respectively. As amateurs, they would make mistakes with a missed string or an out-of-tune key on the piano. But at the conclusion of their playing, we would give them warm applause, thinking they were great.

I have found that these special occasions don't just happen; a successful party is the result of careful planning and organization, and an awareness of just what makes special occasions memorable.

# Planning a Successful Party

In all of my organizational books, I stress the importance of having a plan and making the plan work for you. Once I've decided upon a party, I start making lists of both priorities and details for implementing the list. I create a guest list and purchase invitations that reflect the theme or occasion. Then I plan a menu, along with an appropriate shopping list. I jot down what I need to present the food: tablecloths, napkins, flatware, dishes, glassware, and any special serving pieces that the menu might require. If I have to rent any of these items, I contact a rental company (see the Yellow Pages in your phone book) and make those arrangements.

On another list, I jot down details about flowers, candles, and special decorations, along with any appropriate music or individual touches that help make the occasion special.

I know that if I am well-organized when my guests arrive, they will be more relaxed and can rapidly get into the mood for the happening.

Since food is such a vital part of holiday gatherings, I have included some true-and-tried recipes that go along with each chapter. In some cases, they are ones which I have used successfully over the years. Other recipes were given to me by family and friends, and some come from theme magazines or books. Each one has been kept in its original form (with minor changes to reduce fat content while attempting to keep the delicious taste).

We aren't attempting to make you a gourmet cook who must put in hours and hours of preparation time. And most of the ingredients for our recipes are easily found in the typical grocery store.

Good organization, great guests, good food, and an attractive table setting are not the only keys to creating memorable moments. The most important ingredients are thought and caring. The activities should be fun, the food appealing, and the host should be concerned for those who gather—regardless of the event. Memories are what we celebrate.

Let's start with first things first: "But seek first His kingdom and His righteousness; and all these things shall be added to you" (Matthew 6:33). Each day we need to make the commitment to establish God as number one in our lives. If you have not made the decision to give God the number-one spot in your life, do so today; settle that basic question. Establish your priorities in life, and then the activities of each day will fall together in meaningful sequences.

These homemade memories can be made anywhere that people call home: an apartment, a duplex, one bedroom in a house, a condominium, a college dorm, a mobile home, or an estate. These memories are for all types of families—big or small, headed by a single parent or a married couple, with or without children. Wherever home is, you can create memories that will be treasured.

---

*Today is the last day of your past and the first day of your future. There's no better time to begin "making memories" with your precious family—*Shirley Dobson.

# 2

## Birthdays

"*THUS IT CAME ABOUT* on the third day, which was Pharaoh's birthday, that he made a feast for all his servants" (Genesis 40:20).

**When Observed:** On the person's date of birth
**Earliest Observance:** Pharaoh in Genesis 40:20

The practice of marking an individual's exact date of birth came into existence only with the recording of time by a fixed calendar. Originally, birthdays were not celebrated by commoners. It has only been in recent times that general populations have celebrated individual birthdays. In Europe and America an individual's birthday is celebrated with a family dinner or a party with friends and the custom of giving gifts. This is an important occasion, especially for a child.

Different countries share unique traditions. In general, a birthday is a specific time each year to give special praise and recognition to the person whose birth we celebrate. One way to make this a special tradition is to take time out of our busy schedules to do something different. Maybe write a message:

This is your day!
Good news! Psalm 139:13-16 (TEV):
    You created every part of me; you put me together
    in my mother's womb. I praise you because you are to

be feared; all you do is strange and wonderful. I know it
with all my heart. When my bones were being formed,
carefully put together in my mother's womb, when I was
growing there in secret, you knew that I was there—you
saw me before I was born. The days allotted to me had
all been recorded in your book, before any of them ever
began.

Birthdays are always made special in our home—maybe because when I was growing up they never were. I remember when I
was 12, I gave myself my first birthday party. My mother was trying to make ends meet after my father's death by opening a small
dress shop. We lived in three rooms behind the store, and mother
was always busy with customers, doing alterations and book work.
Birthday parties were not a priority. I had always wanted a party, so
I did it myself. I gave out invitations, cleaned the house, baked
a cake, cut flowers, and put up streamers. My friends came and
brought presents. I was so embarrassed that I hid in the closet and
wouldn't come out. The adult in me could plan the party and organize the attention. I wanted it, but when it came, it was over-
whelming. It was then that I decided to make birthdays special for
my children someday.

Many times during the year we would talk about our birthdays.
I would always (and still do) make the children's favorite meal. Almost every year they would have some kind of birthday celebration.

I'll never forget when our Jenny had her seventh birthday. Of
any of us in the family, Jenny loved a party the most and still does,
even though she is now a grown woman with three children of her
own. We planned for her to invite ten of her closest friends from
church and school. She took her invitations and hand-carried
them to each person. But unknown to me, she not only invited her
ten friends, but also verbally invited anyone who even looked like
a friend. After the mothers dropped off their children for the party,
we ended up with 24 children. The 12 cupcakes we cut in half, and
the children scrambled for the prizes. It was crazy, but that was our

Jenny. She couldn't hurt the other children's feelings by not inviting them, so she invited her whole class. It was most definitely a
party—and truly a memory for Mom.

Parties with themes can be a lot of fun and will flow well because you have a definite plan. When my Bob turned 50, we had a
surprise fiftieth BEARthday party—our theme was teddy bears.
The invitations were teddy bears cut out of brown construction paper that said, "*You're invited to Bob's 50th BEARthday.* Bring a teddy
dressed in a costume to depict Bob."

The plans took quite a while and, when I got home, Bob was
really upset that I had been gone so long. "Where have you been?
The phones have rung off the hook; the UPS delivery came. People
came by for orders. It's really hard for me to handle this all by myself." Well, I couldn't tell him the truth, or I'd give the whole surprise
away. But I sure wanted to say, "I was at Jenny's making *your* birthday invitations." He never caught on, and the party was a surprise.

I filled the room with helium balloons tied to each chair. The
centerpiece consisted of a potted plant in a basket with small cloth
teddy bears I had stuffed with fiberfill then glue-gunned onto bam-
boo spears purchased from the Oriental section of the market. I
tied three balloons on the handle of the plant basket. A friend
made baseball hats with a teddy bear on the bill for each man. I
had white T-shirts silk-screened with a big teddy bear and "Bob's
50 BEARthday 1984," which everyone wore to the party.

The high school our children attended had two Poly Bears as
their mascots. Jenny, being a cheerleader, called the school asking if we could borrow the two mascots for Bob's BEARthday
party. They felt it was an honor to be invited. So we had bears all
over the place. When Bob arrived at the party, the two Poly Bears
slipped out to escort him in carrying a dozen helium balloons. I
wish I had a video of that scene. It was *great!* In they came. We
all yelled, "Surprise BEARthday, Bob!" But that was just the
beginning.

After dinner and honey buns, each couple stood up with their
dressed teddy bear and explained why they dressed it that way. All

depicted different qualities of Bob's friendship. We had the Preppie Bear wearing saddle shoes. Bob most generally wears saddle shoes. We had the football referee with a black-and-white shirt and whistle around his neck. Bob spent many years refereeing high school football games to supplement our incomes. We had a teddy studying his Bible wearing glasses. Bob has taught adult and college Bible studies most of our 39 years of marriage. Our daughter and son-in-law brought a gray-haired Papa bear wearing glasses since they have made Bob a grandpa. On and on the display of teddy bears came.

A longtime friend, Bob Swanson, wrote Bob a song and entertained the guests with his guitar music and song. We all nearly keeled over with laughter. The local newspaper got wind of the affair and came and took pictures and wrote an article, which all of Riverside viewed the next week. So the whole world knew Bob Barnes had turned 50. It was a memory to last a lifetime.

Our daughter gave her husband a surprise birthday party the first year they were married, and everyone came dressed in pink—even the men wore pink shirts. It was a simple thing to do, and yet it made the party a bit different and very creative.

Here's an idea for the working woman. I went to a surprise fortieth birthday party for my friend Yoli Brogger. We all met at 5:00 A.M. at her neighbor's home dressed in our nighties and robes. The working gals put robes over their clothes. We walked down the middle of the street with dawn barely on the horizon, through her front door, down the hall, and into her bedroom yelling, "Surprise!" She was in shock—hair tousled, no makeup. She thought it was a dream as 20 silly mid-life ladies stood at her feet and sang "Happy Birthday." We had such a fun time drinking tea and coffee with birthday cake and fruit at 5:30 A.M. By 7:00 A.M. the presents were opened and the party was over.

Another of our much-loved friends had her surprise birthday party last for 40 days with lunches and brunches provided.

Birthdays don't have to be a surprise. Our son, Brad, isn't big on birthday parties as such. He enjoys quiet family times with favorite foods and warm conversation. We acknowledge that and occasionally have a small party for him.

Other birthday ideas that might enrich your day:

1. *Birthday flag or banner*—Design and create a birthday flag or banner for each family member. Make this flag or banner out of cloth that will last (canvas is great). Place on it the person's favorite colors, sports interests, school activities, hobbies, etc. Fly the flag from sunup to sundown on a pole or hang the banner from a special hook on a fence or on the side of the house. You might even have a special flag raising and lowering ceremony and sing a favorite song, yell a cheer, or dance a dance to start the day off right.

2. *Birthday cup and/or plate*—Designate a special cup and/or plate to be used by the members of your family only on their birthdays. It's a great way to give special honor and recognition to that birthday person.

3. *A song at 9:02 A.M.*—On June 8, a friend of ours was born at 9:02 A.M., and at the exact time each year her family sings "Happy Birthday" to her. In college, she was sure to be in the dorm at that exact time, because she knew she would receive the traditional call. Even today, though married and living in another state, she still looks forward to that traditional call. She now has started the same tradition with her two sons.

4. *Love notes for Daddy*—While baking Dad's favorite German chocolate cake one year, we decided to do something special for him. We wanted to give him a gift that would last all year. We took small strips of paper and made coupons that Dad could redeem anytime during the year. We placed these in a small, colorful tray that he could set on his dresser. We wrote things like:

   ✦ Good for one back rub—Jenny

   ✦ Good for one fried-chicken dinner—Mom

   ✦ Good for one extra hug and kiss—Brad

5. A *special beginning*—Plan special activities for the honored birthday person. Some might be:

   ✦ Choose one gift and put it at the birthday person's place at the breakfast table to be opened as soon as his or her day begins.

   ✦ Have the birthday person plan the menu for supper (or you might even let the person choose a special restaurant if the budget permits).

   ✦ Have clean linens on the birthday person's bed and clean towels in the bathroom.

6. *Weekend celebration*—Try to celebrate your children's birthdays at a hotel that has a pool, game room, and nearby restaurants. Just getting together as a family creates many fond stories for the memory bank.

7. *Creative gifts*—

   ✦ Tickets to the zoo
   ✦ A beach towel
   ✦ New socks
   ✦ Art supplies

8. *Un-birthday party*—Pick a date during the warm summer months to have a party with all the birthday trimmings. Who is it for? No one special—just a reason for family and friends to get together.

9. *Adopted birthday*—If you have an adopted child, you might want to let that child have two birthdays—one for the actual birthday, and another celebrating the day on which he or she came into your home. This second day makes the child feel a special part of a very special family.

10. A happy *"half"* birthday—Make a big deal celebrating your child's half birthday. You can carry out the theme by having a half

birthday cake, a half glass of punch, half of a birthday card, etc. Be creative in carrying through the "half" theme.

11. *Birthday letters in a shoe box*—When I was 21, my mother presented me with a very special birthday gift. Wrapped beautifully in a shoe box were 21 letters Mom had written to me. She had started this tradition the first year of my life, and it was her secret until my twenty-first birthday.

    The letters contained memories of the funny things I said and did over the years, the struggles during the teenage situations, times we spent together, differences we had, tears shed, and the love we enjoyed. Thanks, Mom, for the best gift in 21 years.

12. *Theme parties*—At our youngest grandchild's (Bradley Joe II) second birthday, we planned a birthday party around animals. We contacted a lady who brought a "petting zoo" to our home— a pony, a calf, two ducks, two pigs, four goats, and a baby lamb. This group of city children had a wonderful day experiencing a little bit of farm life. Maria and Brad carried out the theme beautifully by coordinating the cups, plates, napkins, banners, and streamers to reflect farm animals. My, the flashbulbs went off all afternoon! Upon leaving the event, the parents said that without a doubt this was the most fun that they had ever had at a child's birthday party.

13. *Games that break the ice*—

    ✦ Have the guests tell their first name and a word that describes themselves using the first letter of their name. (Example: My name is Christine and I am cute. My name is Chad and I'm charismatic. My name is Bevan and I am believable. My name is Bradley Joe and I'm brave.)

    ✦ Have guests tell their first name and when they are going on a vacation and how they are going to get there using the first letter of their name. (Example: My name is Maria and I'm going to Maryland by motorboat.)

+ Have guests tell their first name and their favorite beverage using the first letter of their name. (Example: My name is Barbara and I like berry juice.)

+ Put 20 wooden clothespins on a clothes hanger. Have the guests remove a clothespin and tell their first names and something special about themselves each time they remove a pin. Guests can only use one hand, and if they drop a pin, they must stop. The person who holds the most pins wins a door prize.

+ Have guests introduce themselves by telling one of the following about themselves:

  • Their favorite color

  • Their favorite TV program

  • Their favorite food

  • When they were born, etc.

+ Have guests tell their first names and punch their weight into a calculator. They then guess the total weight of all the guests at the party. The person with the closest guess wins a door prize. (If you give prizes to your guests at a birthday party, make sure that every child goes home with at least one prize.)

14. *A rented birthday party*—In many communities there are businesses which provide birthday parties for a fee per guest. They supply everything you need, plus provide food and a birthday cake with punch. Some businesses even throw in a clown or two.

15. *Birthday outings*—Birthdays are a great time to plan a trip to the park, a beach, or the mountains. Or you might go boating or sailing. Use your imagination to create that most unusual birthday theme. Don't get in a rut of doing the same thing each year.

16. A *tenth-birthday box*—On our grandchildren's tenth birthday, they get a big box (like a dishwasher or refrigerator box) full of ten gifts. This is a special benchmark of their lives. We spray-paint the box their favorite color and tie a big ribbon around it with the child's name written in huge letters on the outside of the package. One of the gifts is an envelope with ten new, crisp one-dollar bills (get these at the bank). In addition, we give them nine other gifts that they may have requested for their birthday.

    After all the festivities, they get to play in the big box. This is the most fun of all their gifts. They can play in this big box for hours. It soon becomes a plane, a boat, or a train. After it is all over, Bob and I look at each other and say, "Why didn't we just give them a big box to play with?"

17. A *gift for the future*—A tremendous grandparent gift to a grandchild is to go to your local bank and purchase a U.S. Treasury bond made payable to the birthday girl/boy. They will really appreciate that gift when they get older and think of college.

18. *Annual birthday interview*—This acts as a great chronological record for your child's development:

    ✦ On each child's birthday, record on an audio- or videocassette an interview with him/her. Ask the birthday person to describe special memories about the past year—happy times, sad moments, fun things that happened, and other meaningful experiences.

    ✦ Add to the recording every year at the time of each birthday.

    ✦ After each interview, play back the previous years' conversations.

19. *"Do-it-yourself" birthday party*—

    ✦ Plan a birthday party for six or eight children, ages ten and younger.

- Look in your cookbook for a yummy gingerbread cookie recipe and assemble the ingredients needed to make it, along with the necessary utensils.

- When the guests arrive, let them help you make gingerbread kids cookies. Each child can then take home the cookie he or she made.

20. *Instant party for a loved one away from home—*

- Bake cookies and arrange them in a box with packets of fruit punch mix, party napkins, and paper cups.

- Wrap the box in birthday paper with a card explaining that you are sending an "instant party."

- Finish with an outer wrapping of brown paper and mail to that special birthday person.

- Instruct the person not to open the package until the day of his or her birthday.

21. *Birthday balloon walk*—Inflate a number of bright balloons. Divide the group of children into two or more equal teams. At the signal, each person must carry the balloon between his knees to the goal line and back. If the balloon breaks, he must come back for a new one and start over. The first team to finish is the winner. A large balloon for each team member would be an appropriate prize.

    *Variations:* 1) Play this as an individual competition, using a stopwatch to time each competitor. The one with the shortest time is the winner. 2) Set up an obstacle course for players to walk through on their way to the goal line.

22. *Questions and answers*—Have guests fill in answers for all the items below. Give them a hint that all answers will contain the words *red*, *white*, or *blue*.

1. Stop signal . . . . . . . . . . . . . . . . . . . . . . . . . . . red light

2. President's home . . . . . . . . . . . . . . . . . . . . White House

3. Fib . . . . . . . . . . . . . . . . . . . . . . . . . . . . . . . . white lie

4. Nursery rhyme . . . . . . . . . . . . . . . . . . . Little Boy Blue

5. Porter at train station . . . . . . . . . . . . . . . . . . . . redcap

6. Moby Dick . . . . . . . . . . . . . . . . . . . . . . . . white whale

7. Architect's plan . . . . . . . . . . . . . . . . . . . . . . . blueprint

8. Famous song by Irving Berlin . . . . . . . White Christmas

9. Luncheon special . . . . . . . . . . . . . . . . . . . . blue plate

10. Depressing workday . . . . . . . . . . . . . . . . . Blue Monday

## Birthday Parties on a Budget

✦ Keep the party small. A good rule to follow is invite the same number of children as the number of years in your child's age.

✦ Get a family member or a babysitter to help (let grandparents be guests, not helpers).

✦ Have a backup plan for an outdoor party in case of rain.

✦ Use color comics for decorations and cartoon bedsheets as tablecloths. Crayons make nice party favors, and kids can use them to decorate white paper tablecloths and paper plates. Children's toys make good decorations: stuffed animals with party hats, a dump truck holding chips or cookies.

✦ Use creativity with party favors. Wrap peanut-butter play dough or homemade play dough in a plastic bag, tying it shut with a ribbon. Kids can decorate lunch bags and then fill them up as they go on a candy, peanut, or penny hunt.

+ Don't plan the party at mealtime; it's more expensive. From 2 to 4 P.M. is a good time.

+ Plan activities, but don't expect the children to play all the games. If the kids are having fun, don't interrupt. If they're bored, bring in a new game.

+ Have your cake and be able to afford it, too. If a homemade cake has frosting and the child gets to pick the flavors, he's happy. Licorice, candy, or animal crackers make good sheet cake decorations.

+ Don't serve blue icing, red punch, or other things that stain or make children overactive.

+ Pick a party theme. Some ideas: beach party, tea party, costume party, dinosaur party, frontier party, scavenger hunt, backyard camp out, detective party.

+ An artist party can be fun. Get five or more large boxes for the children to paint or color and make into churches, homes, or cars.

+ For children ages five to seven, try a soap bubble party and invite a storyteller.

+ Beware of hiring clowns or big characters for toddler parties. Clowns are inappropriate for children younger than three, because small children get frightened. With children ages three and older, it is suggested that the host ask how the clown will dress. Clowns that wear makeup and colorful costumes but no frightening wigs are better. By eliminating the wig, the clown might be able to get the children to stand and talk to him, or at least not run.

+ Remember that a party for a child's first couple of birthdays is really for family and friends to celebrate a new life. The child doesn't understand what's going on.

+ Don't make your children share their presents.

+ Save opening the presents till the end. It's a good way to slow down a party.

+ Have a specific ending time for the party. Playing a video is a nice way to keep stragglers who are waiting for rides home occupied. Once everyone is gone, take a few minutes for some hugs and talk about the party. Save the cleanup for later.

+ If some members of your family live far away or can't come to the party, make a video recording and send it to them. They will love seeing the party, and it will help your family stay in touch.

# 3

*Valentine's Day*

"THIS IS MY COMMANDMENT, that you love one another, just as I have loved you" (John 15:12).

**When Observed:** February 14
**Earliest Observance:** Middle Ages

February 14 has become special in America, as for one day we return our hearts to love. My earliest recollection of this special day is from when I was in elementary school. With great anticipation and thoughtful selection, I chose and signed that special card for that somewhat secret sweetheart.

Many decades later I still look at February 14 as a special time for expressing love and affection to those special to me. Everyone knows that Valentine's Day is that day of the year when friends and lovers express affection for one another with cards, candy, and flowers, or through whatever means their imaginations can find. The symbols for this day are hearts, cupids, and arrows. Red, white, and pink are this day's colors.

No one is quite sure who St. Valentine was. The early lists of church martyrs reveal at least three people named Valentine, each of whom had his feast day on February 14.

Various legends have come down to us, too. Valentine was said to have been imprisoned and, while there, he cured the jailer's daughter of blindness. Another story, in an attempt to associate

Valentine more closely with Valentine's Day, has him falling in love with the jailer's daughter and sending her a letter which he signed, "From your Valentine."

In the Middle Ages throughout Europe, there was a belief that birds mated on February 14. This belief that birds chose their mates on Valentine's Day led to the idea that boys and girls would do the same. Even at the turn of the twentieth century in the hills of the Ozarks, folks thought that birds and rabbits started the mating season on February 14—a day which was for people in this region not only Valentine's Day, but Groundhog Day as well.

Some people even give credit for this day to the early Roman feast day of Lupercalia, which was celebrated in February in honor of the pastoral god Lupercus—a Roman version of the Greek god Pan. During this festival the names of young women were put into a box. Youths then drew the names, and the boys and girls so matched would be considered partners for the year which began in March.

The English settlers in the New World brought their Valentine customs with them. Prior to the eighteenth century, original valentine cards of a certain homeliness and simplicity had been exchanged among some colonists. But after 1723, the custom really began to grow with the impact from England valentine writers.

Commercial valentines came out about 1800, and by 1840 were becoming sophisticated. The reduction of postal rates brought about a great increase in the number of valentines sent, and printed valentines became popular. Today, valentine greetings are made for sending to nearly everyone—friend, relative, and sweetheart alike. Valentine's Day is second only to Christmas in the number of greetings sent in the United States.

## Christian Activities

As Christians we can certainly celebrate this holiday with our families and friends better if we look at the Bible and see how many times love is used to express the relationship between God and mankind. Our faith is built upon our proper understanding and expression of love. Below are some Scriptures that express God's love to us. May we appreciate our scriptural heritage and through this understanding put into practice a true expression of love to those around us.

Deuteronomy 6:5—"And you shall love the LORD your God with all your heart and with all your soul and with all your might."

Psalm 18:1—"I love Thee, O LORD, my strength."

Psalm 116:1—"I love the LORD, because He hears my voice and my supplications."

Psalm 145:20—"The LORD keeps all who love Him."

Proverbs 8:17—"I love those who love me; and those who diligently seek me will find me."

Romans 8:28—"And we know that God causes all things to work together for good to those who love God."

## Valentine Ideas

On Valentine's Day we have an opportunity to give of ourselves in love. Homemade valentines with lace, ribbon, craft paper, and glue are almost a lost art. Anyone, even the least artistic person, can create a lovely valentine, but you can also buy prepackaged valentines.

"Good for" coupons make a great valentine for anyone—from children to grandparents. The coupons could include:

- one evening of babysitting
- two hours of yard work or weed-pulling
- one hour of ironing, sewing, or mending
- the preparation of one meal

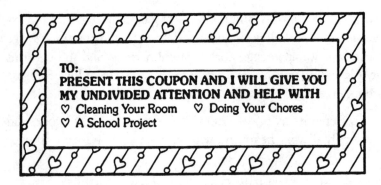

TO: _____
**PRESENT THIS COUPON AND I WILL GIVE YOU**
**MY UNDIVIDED ATTENTION AND HELP WITH**
♡ Cleaning Your Room    ♡ Doing Your Chores
♡ A School Project

Give a gift of yourself and your talents as an expression of love. God showed us His love in His Son, Jesus. What an outreach and even a ministry you can create through expressing your love.

Valentine's Day provides children with an opportunity to give from their hearts. One mother in our neighborhood had cookie-baking day with her three girls. They frosted heart-shaped cookies and topped them with jelly beans, coconut, raisins, and nuts and then made up small paper plates filled with loving, homemade cookies and took them to each family on the block. This same idea carried over to other holidays as well: tree-shaped cookies for Christmas, turkey-shaped for Thanksgiving, and cross-shaped for Easter. What this mother taught her girls was more important than how to make cookies. She taught her daughters how to give as Christ gave to us.

Don't think it's "sissy" to give plants or flowers to a man. One wife shared how she sent her husband a bouquet of flowers at work. He wasn't an executive in a high-rise office building, either. It was a sacrifice for her, and she saved for a long time to do it. The other workers all stopped to see who was getting those beautiful flowers. They didn't make fun of him, but admired him and the relationship he and his wife had. If flowers seem a bit too much, try a balloon or box of candy, or pack him a fancy lunch with a heart-shaped sandwich. Write love notes between the lettuce and tomato. He'll find and love them—and hopefully won't eat them.

Valentine's week is a good time to pull out wedding photos and honeymoon pictures. Use this time to reminisce and to recall special memories.

I save my leftover red Christmas candles for Valentine's week, and we have candlelight breakfasts or dinners, children and all. Red napkins and place mats and white lace doilies make nice place settings. A paper or fabric heart wreath can be put on your front door or mailbox the week before Valentine's Day as a sure sign of love and welcome to friends, neighbors, and family.

Valentine's Day gives us an excellent opportunity to reach out to others—to send a note, deliver a handmade valentine, or give a basket of homemade goodies.

Perhaps an apology is due to a friend or family member. Now is the perfect time to settle those differences. A note of apology in love could open the doors for good feelings in the future.

## Additional Valentine's Day Ideas

1. *Lend a helping hand*—Make a large red heart with white lace doilies on the edges. In the middle write the words, "I did it because I love you." Take the card and place it next to something you did to show your love for that person:
   + a bed that has been made
   + dishes washed and put away
   + a carpet that has been vacuumed

2. *How Mom and Dad met*—With the family around, have Dad and Mom tell the story of their first date and courtship. They may include:
   + How and where they met
   + Activities and places they enjoyed while dating
   + When they fell in love
   + What qualities attracted them to one another

◆ How Dad proposed

◆ Humorous stories about their courtship

Have Dad and Mom show pictures of themselves when they were young. As a nice touch, Dad can show the family how he kissed Mom the very first time.

3. *Valentine notes*—Bake a cake and put little notes in it. The children will love this and look forward to it each year. Write some love notes, positive messages, or short Bible verses on strips of paper, fold the papers into small squares, wrap them in foil, and place the notes throughout the cake batter. When the children get a piece of cake, they will love to see if there's a note inside.

4. *Love messages*—

◆ Write notes of love to *each* member of your family.

◆ Tell them why you love them and appreciate them. Be specific!

◆ Tuck notes in their lunchboxes, notebooks, or briefcases, along with special valentine treats.

◆ Call your spouse today and say how much you love him or her.

◆ Send a fax expressing your love.

◆ With red lipstick write "I love you" on your spouse's side of the bathroom mirror.

5. *A dinner by candlelight*—Cook a special meal and eat it on your good dishes with your prettiest glasses and serving ware in the formal dining room (if you have one). Prepare a special dessert with the children's names on the different pieces or a large cake with a special Valentine's Day message. Select for each of the children a special valentine card—even add a few of your own special words. You might even send out a special invitation to

your dinner party a few days ahead of time. It is a good opportunity for the family to dress up. This works best when Dad can help with the preparations.

Keep the children out of the dining room until they are brought in blindfolded. As they take off their blindfolds, their eyes will become large with excitement at seeing this special dinner setting for the first time. During the meal, take turns expressing how important each member is to the family. Let the children know how special they are to Mom and Dad. (By the way, take the phone off the hook.)

6. *Valentine treasure hunt*—

- ✦ Buy a package of inexpensive children's valentines.

- ✦ Write a different love note on each of 10 to 15 cards, or write one word per card to form a message of love.

- ✦ Hide the cards throughout the house, in the car, or in other suitable places.

- ✦ Give a written clue on the outside of each envelope directing your "Valentine" to the next card.

- ✦ Include a small love gift with the last valentine.

7. *Make a heart-shaped cake*—Just bake a round and a square cake. Face the square one toward you, with the point forward like a playing card diamond. Slice the round cake in half and position the two halves against the diamond's uppermost sides. Frost and serve.

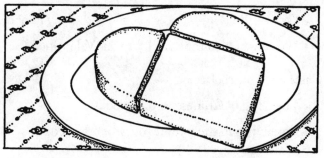

8. *Do-it-yourself candy box*—Instead of giving your sweetie the usual box of chocolates, decorate a box with pretty paper, lace, buttons, and cut-out hearts. Filled with penny candy, it makes a great low-cost gift, and your Valentine can find other uses for the box after the candy is gone.

9. A *valentine dessert*—Our delicious, no-bake Valentine's Day dessert "box" is made of graham crackers—and the "gift" inside is your family's or friend's favorite ice cream or frozen yogurt! Here are the easy instructions:

   ◆ Top a graham cracker square with a scoop of ice cream or frozen yogurt as high and wide as the graham cracker.

   ◆ Place four graham crackers on the sides of the ice cream and press lightly, forming a square. Top with another cracker.

   ◆ Create a "ribbon" and "bow" with a tube of red cake-decorating gel. Freeze until ready to serve.

10. A *candy-bar "hello"*—On a piece of poster board write your Valentine's Day greetings so the candy bar forms part of the message. Some suggested messages might include:

    ◆ "I (mint) to ask you to be my Valentine."

    ◆ "Valentine, you stole a (Big Hunk) of my heart."

    ◆ "I chews (gum) you to be my Valentine."

    ◆ "You're the (Cup 'o Gold) at the end of my rainbow."

    ◆ "I'd run a (Marathon Bar) for you, Valentine."

11. *Chinese fortune cookie notes*—

    ◆ Buy a bag of Chinese fortune cookies.

    ◆ Carefully pull the fortunes out from the cookies with a pair of tweezers.

♦ Cut up small slips of paper and write your *own* messages of love either in one sentence or on several pieces of paper that must be fitted together like a puzzle. Stick the new messages into the cookies. The messages can also be made clever or funny if the occasion dictates.

12. *Have a heart! (or two)*—Make pretty Valentine earrings in a jiffy by following these very easy instructions: Cut two same-sized heart shapes from cardboard. Using red acrylic paint or nail polish, paint both sides of the hearts. Coat the hearts with clear varnish and allow them to dry completely. Glue each heart to an earring base (available at craft and hobby shops).

13. *Cinnamon cocoa*—For a spicy-good winter and Valentine beverage, add a cinnamon-flavored tea bag to a cup of piping-hot cocoa. Steep for a few minutes, then enjoy!

14. *Hair, hair!*—

♦ Make a heart-shaped hair ornament by twisting a red pipe cleaner into a heart. Wrap red or white lace ribbon around it and glue on some glitter. When the glue has dried, attach the heart to a barrette or hair clip.

♦ Save the ribbons from your Valentine's Day gifts. They make perfect hair bows and headbands.

15. *Pink pancakes*—When the family comes to breakfast on Valentine's Day, have pink pancakes already prepared. Just add a little red food coloring to the batter. The children will love it!

16. *Heart sandwiches*—In preparing sandwiches for family members as they go to school and work, take either a large heart-shaped cookie cutter or with a knife shape your bread into a heart. They will love the surprise when they unwrap their sandwiches during the lunch hour. Throw in some chocolate candy kisses for dessert.

17. *Homemade valentines*—Make your own valentines for family members. The handmade ones are still the best.

   ✦ Cut an 8½" x 11" sheet of construction paper in half.

   ✦ Fold each half in half (each full sheet will make two cards).

   ✦ Decorate the cover with hearts, pictures, lace, doilies, ribbons, etc.

   ✦ Compose a poem or verse for your loved one, or write a short essay on "This Is What You Mean to Me" or "You're Something Special Because . . ."

   ✦ Copy the message inside your card.

   ✦ Envelopes to fit this size of card can be purchased at stationery stores or can be made by hand.

18. *Fun food tips*—Use a heart-shaped cookie cutter to create fun Valentine's Day treats for your children. Here's how:

   *Breakfast:* Toast bread, then cut it into heart shapes with the cookie cutter. (Don't cut the slices of bread before toasting, or you may have difficulty removing them from the toaster.)

   *Lunch:* Cut bread or toast into slice-size heart shapes for Valentine's Day sandwiches. Note: Use the trimmings to make bread crumbs in a blender or food processor. Freeze the crumbs for use in casseroles and stuffing.

19. *Wrap it up*—Red or pink shopping bags in good condition can be recycled as Valentine gift-wrapping paper. Just cut the handles off the bag and carefully cut the bottom open. On one side, cut the bag from top to bottom, then smooth out the paper.

20. *Valentine cupcakes*—You can make heart-shaped cupcakes easily by using your favorite cupcake recipe. Place paper baking cups in a muffin tin. Put a marble or small ball of foil in each cup between the paper liner and pan. This makes a heart-shaped

mold in which to cook cupcakes. Pour batter and bake as usual. Don't fill cups too full or you will lose the heart-shaped effect.

21. *Flowerpot centerpiece*—To make a pretty table decoration, you will need four flowerpots of graduating sizes and an assortment of live plants or silk flowers, whichever you prefer. Stack the flowerpots according to size, placing the largest on the bottom and the smallest on top. Arrange the plants or silk flowers in the top flowerpot and around the edges of the other three pots.

22. *A special grandparents' valentine*—Have your children decorate a red construction-paper heart. Cut out a heart shape from the middle of the valentine. Glue your children's school pictures or other recent photos into the heart shape. If the children make one each Valentine's Day, their grandparents will build a collection of special valentines over the years.

23. *Valentine card construction party*—Start a week ahead of time to gather all the materials and supplies. Unfold one or two card tables and lay out an old sheet or tablecloth to cover the table surface (place in an area of the home where the table can be left up for the week). The family can have a fun time constructing their own very special valentines—a great activity to do before or after school (in lieu of television) or after dinner. Mom and Dad can even get into the swing of things.

24. *A special valentine for Mom*—Husbands and children need to get together and think up something special for Mom. Compose a card that reflects how you love her. Give her a small, inexpensive gift. Hubby might want to call from work to whisper a love message to that special lady in his life. Send or take home a bouquet of flowers or a potted plant.

25. *Valentine tea party*—One mom on Valentine's Day makes a special tea party for her children and their friends. They place at each end of the table Raggedy Ann and Andy. She uses her best dishes and cloth napkins. The other moms are invited,

but they sit in the kitchen out of the way. It's first-class for the children and a great idea for teens, too!

26. *Beloved silhouettes—*

+ Use a slide projector or Viewmaster to project the head profile silhouette of each person in the family onto a blank wall. A bright lamp with the shade removed also provides a good light source.

+ Hold poster board against the wall and trace the silhouette with a broad-tipped pen or marker.

+ Cut out each silhouette.

+ Cut a heart shape from a sheet of red construction paper or poster board larger than the size of the silhouette.

+ Paste each silhouette on a separate heart and display them along a hallway or send them to grandparents for valentines.

*Hint:* A heart-shaped paper doily may be pasted under the silhouette, using a contrasting color. For instance, use a red heart with a white doily placed on it. Then paste the black silhouette on top of the doily.

## Romance Is About the Little Things

Valentine's Day is not automatically the most romantic day of the year. It's there on the calendar, but you have to recognize it and act upon it. It doesn't happen in a void. Here are some additional ideas that will make your day very special:

+ Instead of giving roses, this year try something different:
  • Buy a different kind of flower.
  • Write a love letter.

- Take a love basket to your spouse at work and surprise him or her with a special lunch.

- Do something unique, quirky, or touching.

- Write a poem, or copy one from a book of poetry.

- Fax a poem to your mate at the office (it's okay if someone in the office sees it first—they will know that you are a special person).

- Send a bunch of helium balloons to your mate at his or her job.

+ For future reference: Buy an extra bag of Valentine conversation heart candies and save them for use six months later as a surprise.

+ Keep your eyes open for pre-Valentine's Day articles in magazines and newspapers. Rip out the articles, circle the best ideas, and plan accordingly. (And don't forget to keep those articles for future reference!) File them in a manila folder with the heading "Valentine's Day."

+ Mail him one Valentine's Day card—or mail him 20! Make a huge card. Send a musical greeting card—available in most card shops for just a few dollars.

+ Use kids' valentines. Purchase a whole box full of silly puns and clichés, all for a couple of dollars.

  - Mail a box full of them.

  - Fill the empty kitchen sink with them.

  - Fill his briefcase with them.

  - Fill her pillow with them.

  - Tape them all over her car.

  - Mail one-a-day for a month.

◆ Send her a box filled with Valentine conversation heart candies—a big box.

◆ Use Valentine conversation heart candies to spell out a romantic message to her. Leave it on the kitchen table or paste it to a piece of construction paper.

◆ Replace all the Cheerios in the box with Valentine conversation hearts.

◆ Turn Valentine's Day into a real holiday with your spouse: Take the day off work. Spend the day in bed. Go to the movies. Go out to dinner. Go dancing. Take a drive. Make love. Go for a stroll.

◆ Send custom valentines of ribbon and lace, tubes filled with heart-shaped confetti or chocolate hearts, heart-shaped baskets filled with hand-painted notes, or anything else you can think of. (These items are available from Ann Fiedler Creations at (310) 838-1857, or write to 10544 West Pico Boulevard, West Los Angeles, CA 90064.)

◆ Create a Valentine's Day concert, just for the two of you. Record an hour's worth of your favorite romantic music. Print a program. List the song titles, along with some personal commentary about the significance of each song to you, or why particular songs remind you of him or her. Send your spouse an invitation to the concert. Dress for the event. Serve sparkling cider and cheese.

◆ Write "I love you" on the bathroom mirror with a piece of soap.

◆ Write your mate a note, poem, or letter on one sheet of paper. Cut it into puzzle-shaped pieces. Mail all the pieces to your sweetheart in an envelope—or mail one puzzle piece a day for a week.

+ Men, think early and send away for a catalog of beautiful Victorian calling cards, stationery, and note cards for that special lady in your life. Contact: English Garden Press, 557 Mary Esther Cutoff, Ft. Walton Beach, Florida 32548; (904) 664-9127 or fax (904) 664-2571.

## Prescriptions for Romance

+ Compliment your mate. Repeat every four to six hours.

+ Say "I love you" at least three times today. Repeat dosage every day for the rest of your life.

+ The unasked-for gift is most appreciated. The surprise gift is most cherished.

+ Pick a wildflower bouquet.

+ Run your hands and feet under very warm water before coming to bed.

+ Hug at least ten times today. Watch out—it's habit-forming.

+ Kidnap your mate! Blindfold her, drive her around town until she is lost; then tell her where you are going: to a movie, to the theater, to a restaurant, skating, or to a ball game.

+ Hide 25 little "I love you because..." cards all over the house. Write short, romantic notes on index cards, Post-It Notes, or construction paper cut into little hearts. Then hide the notes everywhere: in the *TV Guide*, in pants pockets, in desk drawers, in socks, under magazines, behind pillows, in the tub, in the refrigerator, in the freezer, in the medicine cabinet, in books, in her briefcase, in his car, in the silverware drawer. Some of these notes may remain hidden for months—or even years. So much the better!

## ❦ Heart-Smart Cocoa Kisses

Light as air, low-fat cookies for you and your Valentine:

*Ingredients:*

| | |
|---|---|
| 2 egg whites | 3 tablespoons cocoa |
| ¼ teaspoon cream of tartar | ¾ teaspoon almond extract |
| ⅛ teaspoon salt | ⅓ cup finely chopped almonds |
| ⅔ cup sugar | |

*About two hours before serving:*

1. Preheat oven to 200°. Line 2 large cookie sheets with foil. In small bowl with mixer at high speed, beat egg whites, cream of tartar, and salt until soft peaks form. At high speed, gradually beat in sugar, 2 tablespoons at a time, beating well after each addition. At low speed, beat in cocoa and almond extract until blended. Fold in almonds, reserving 1 tablespoon.

2. Drop mixture by slightly rounded tablespoonfuls onto cookie sheets. Sprinkle tops with reserved almonds.

3. Bake 1 hour and 15 minutes or until set. Cool the cookie sheets on wire racks for 10 minutes. With a metal spatula, carefully loosen and remove kisses from foil; cool completely on wire racks. Store in tightly covered container. Makes about 2 dozen kisses.

# 4

## Easter

"HE IS NOT HERE, but He has risen" (Luke 24:6).

**When Observed:** On the Sunday following the first full moon after the vernal equinox (sometime between March 22 and April 25)

**Earliest Observance:** Second century

Being brought up in the Jewish faith, I had no early experiences with or recollections of Easter in my childhood. I did have a stuffed Easter bunny, colored eggs, a new dress, and new shoes, but I didn't really observe the religious aspects of Easter until I met and married my husband, Bob. At that time I began to realize that Easter has a much more powerful message than what I had experienced. The symbols for Easter are the resurrection-cross and lilies, and the colors are pastels and purple.

I became aware that no holy day or festival in the Christian year compares in importance with Easter Sunday. That Jesus Christ was resurrected after having suffered and died is the belief most central to the Christian faith. Christians believe that by His dying, Jesus accomplished a reconciliation between God and man. The apostle Paul says:

> Now if Christ is preached, that He has been raised
> from the dead, how do some among you say that there

is no resurrection of the dead? But if there is no resurrection of the dead, not even Christ has been raised; and if Christ has not been raised, then our preaching is vain, and your faith also is vain (1 Corinthians 15:12-14).

I also learned in Matthew's Gospel that, after the crucifixion, Joseph of Arimathea placed Jesus in his own tomb and rolled a great stone across the entrance. But the Pharisees and Pilate feared that the disciples might come and steal Jesus' body to fulfill His prophecy: "After three days I will rise again." So the tomb was sealed and a guard was placed around the tomb.

On the third day, Mary Magdalene came to the tomb with Mary the mother of James:

> And behold, a severe earthquake had occurred, for an angel of the Lord descended from heaven and came and rolled away the stone and sat upon it. And his appearance was like lightning, and his garment as white as snow; and the guards shook for fear of him and became like dead men. And the angel answered and said to the women, "Do not be afraid; for I know that you are looking for Jesus who has been crucified. He is not here, for He has risen, just as He said. Come, see the place where He was lying. And go quickly and tell His disciples that He has risen from the dead; and behold, He is going before you into Galilee, there you will see Him; behold, I have told you" (Matthew 28:2-7).

The feast of Easter was well-established by the second century. There was a great deal of controversy over whether the day should be celebrated on a weekday or whether Easter should always be on a Sunday, regardless of date. In A.D. 325, the Council of Nicaea decided that Easter should fall on the Sunday following the first full moon after the vernal equinox. This calculation was made easier when March 21 was chosen as the date of the vernal equinox.

In the early church, the several days called Pascha commemorated the passion, death, and resurrection of Jesus Christ. By the fourth century, Pascha Sunday had become a separate day which commemorated the glorious resurrection.

In Britain, the feast was named Easter after the Anglo-Saxon goddess of spring, Eastre.

Many of the early settlers of America were Puritans or members of Protestant denominations who didn't want anything to do with pagan religious festivals. The celebration of Easter in this country was therefore severely limited. It is well-known that the Puritans in Massachusetts outlawed the celebration of Christmas, and they also tried to play down the observance of Easter as far as possible.

After the Civil War, the message and meaning of Easter began to be more widely celebrated when the story of the resurrection was used by the Presbyterians as a logical inspiration of renewed hope for all those bereaved by the war.

Since then, Easter has become a major religious and secular celebration. Its joyous customs delight children and adults alike. It is a family day when relatives and friends gather after church services for festive dinners or maybe a park picnic, weather permitting.

Easter heralds the beginning of spring and is generally accompanied by a week's vacation from school.

One of the beautiful religious customs of Easter is the dawn service held by many Christian denominations. These services may well have their origin in the biblical text: "But on the first day of the week, at early dawn, they came to the tomb" (Luke 24:1). The outdoor Easter sunrise service was brought to America by Protestant emigrants from Moravia. The first such service in America was held in Bethlehem, Pennsylvania, in 1741.

Many Christians are torn between the religious significance of the biblical account of Christ's birth, death, and resurrection and the pagan and secular thrust given to these holidays. We struggle with the concept of being in the world but not of the world. Easter and Christmas seem to have been diluted over the past few decades. We want to honor the Scriptures, but we are also bombarded with the Easter bunny, dyeing eggs, egg hunts, Easter clothing, etc. One of the ways a family might want to separate the secular from the religious is to celebrate Easter Saturday and do on that day all those activities which don't fall into the religious function of the season and which are the children's "fun" part of Easter.

## Easter Saturday Ideas

1. Decorate and dye your eggs.

2. Hide the eggs in the lawn area of your home or at a friend's home, or go to a park and have an Easter egg hunt. You might even include a "treasure egg" and offer a special prize to the child who discovers it. If your children's ages span several years, you might consider having two separate egg hunts—one for the smaller children and one for the older set.

   This hunt can involve your whole family, plus your neighborhood, and friends, or it can be scaled down to include just you and a child. Don't let the lack of numbers discourage you.

3. Inside your "treasure egg" you might want to hide money, a gift, a candy treat, or a small toy.

4. Try decorating the serving table in spring colors and serving light refreshments after the hunt.

5. You and your neighbors or friends might want to join together and hire a clown or magician to come to the party and entertain the children.

6. There are usually some children who don't find any eggs and others who find more than they can carry. This provides a wonderful opportunity to talk about sharing with others.

7. Have an art project in mind that uses the eggshells when they are peeled from the eggs. Since the shells are colored, cracked,

and in small pieces, they make excellent material for an Easter mosaic. Assemble a large sheet of poster or construction paper, white glue, and assorted colors of broken eggshells. Trace or draw a simple Easter picture onto your piece of paper. Glue the pieces of colored eggshells onto the paper to fill up your drawing.

8. Use a loaf of unsliced bread and cut the top off, leaving the sides and an attached handle for a basket. Hollow out the bread so Easter goodies can be placed inside. Trim with ribbon. Grind the unused bread for bread crumbs. This becomes an Easter bread basket.

9. Personalize your eggs by enclosing Easter messages in the shells. To blow out the raw eggs, use a sharp needle and poke a small hole in the small end of each egg and a larger hole in the big end. Through the larger hole, puncture the egg yolk with the needle. Hold the egg over a bowl and gently blow through the small hole to force the raw egg out of the large hole. Rinse shells carefully and thoroughly.

   Decorate blown-out eggshells with marking pens, ribbon, lace, or watercolor paints. Write messages on small pieces of paper. Roll them up and carefully place them inside the eggs through the larger hole. Your messages could contain something related to the Easter story.

10. *Egg Tips:*

    + If you add two tablespoons of vinegar to the water before cooking your eggs, the egg white from cracked eggs will not leak into the water.

    + Puncture the large end of the eggshell with a needle just before cooking to keep eggs from cracking.

    + Although fresh eggs can be stored in their cartons in the refrigerator for two to three weeks, hard-boiled eggs should be refrigerated when cooled and used within one week.

    + Grate the leftover hard-boiled eggs and place portions in

small freezer bags and freeze for later use. Thawed, they provide an excellent garnish for green salads. Grated eggs taste good creamed over toast or added to casseroles—and even make delicious deviled eggs.

✦ Natural dyes can be put to work at Easter time. You'll have green eggs if you boil them with green grass, red if they're boiled with beets, and yellow if onion skins are in the pot.

11. Double-dipping—Before the Easter bunny became their ambassador, colored eggs were a symbol of springtime. For thousands of years, Ukrainians created elaborately patterned eggs using a wax-resist process. Updated and simplified, the same technique can be used to produce these soft watercolor patterns:

a. To make a striped egg, dye a raw or hard-boiled egg pale yellow (for rich colors, double or triple the proportion of coloring to water recommended on most food-coloring boxes). Let dry.

b. Melt beeswax (available at art-supply stores) in a pot. Dip both ends of the egg in wax to prevent them from absorbing the next color.

c. Place the egg in the green dye for about a minute, then remove and let dry. Dip both ends of the egg deeper in the wax than before, leaving a narrow unwaxed band around the middle of the egg.

d. Place the egg in dark blue to dye the middle stripe. When finished, place the egg in a 250° oven on a cookie sheet lined with waxed paper for about five minutes. Take the egg out and wipe off melted wax with a paper towel. If you used a raw egg, carefully blow out the contents.

To make a half-colored egg, hold an egg partially submerged in a strong dye for about a minute. To create eggs with bands of white, dip-dye both ends, then dip each end deep enough in the wax to cover the dyed areas plus stripes of white beyond them, and proceed as above.

12. You and your family might want to make up a special Easter
    basket for those friends or neighbors who might be in need of
    food, clothing, or even a little touch of special loving.

---

### Little Jelly Beans

Little jelly beans
Tell a story true
A tale of our Father's love
Just for me and you.
GREEN is for the waving palms
BLUE for the skies above
BROWN for the soft earth where
People sat hearing of His love.
A SPECKLED bean for fish and sand
RED for precious wine
And BLACK is for the sin He washed
From your soul and mine.
PURPLE'S for the sadness of
His family and friends
And WHITE is for the glory of the
Day He rose again.
Now you've heard the story
You know what each color means
The story of our Father's love
Told by some jelly beans.
So every morning take a bean
They're really very yummy.
Something for the soul, you see.
And something for the tummy.

—Author unknown

Use Easter Saturday to share the secular activities, and reserve Easter Sunday as the day for celebrating and sharing in the death and resurrection of the Lord Jesus Christ.

## Christian Activities for Easter Sunday

> And these words, which I am commanding you today, shall be on your heart; and you shall teach them diligently to your sons and shall talk of them when you sit in your house and when you walk by the way and when you lie down and when you rise up (Deuteronomy 6:6,7).

1. Plan with your family to attend an Easter morning sunrise service. Starting the week before, you may want to read as a family a little each day in John 12–20 about the story of the life of Christ leading up to the crucifixion and resurrection. This background will make the sunrise service more meaningful to the children.

2. After a light breakfast, attend a regular church service.

3. Easter is a great time to have the extended family together for lunch or dinner. Rather than one family having full responsibility for food preparation, you might suggest a potluck with various families bringing different parts of the menu. Some families also rotate the location to a different home each year. This way no one family has the continuous responsibility of hosting the meal year after year.

4. When the immediate family is not available for celebration at Thanksgiving and/or Christmas, you might use Easter as the holiday when you come together as a total family. You could even use the symbols of Christmas with an Easter flair. Be creative and see how exciting you can make the theme.

5. Around the dining table you could have the Easter story written out and attached to the name tags or napkin rings. Before blessing the food, have various members of the family read their Scripture and share what that verse means to them.

6. Have your children prepare a drama depicting a segment of the Easter story, and let the other children or adults try to guess what segment they are portraying.

7. Before the day is over, prepare and share a family communion using bread or crackers and grape juice.

Prepare a loaf of bread (unleavened, if possible) and a cup of grape juice so that the family can share in the "one bread" and "one cup." (Read Matthew 26:17-30.) If it is your conviction that only a clergyman can administer communion, you might invite one of your church's staff members to join you in this part of the celebration.

As you take a piece of bread, share with the next person what is so special to you about Easter. Then in a prayer of thanksgiving, express how special Jesus is to you and your family. You might even have several members of the family pray. As in this passage of Scripture, you could close with a song. (If everyone isn't familiar with the song, print copies of the words.)

8. Easter story eggs—To remind your family of the Easter story, prepare an Easter basket with 12 plastic eggs that can be opened. On the outside of the egg write a number (1 to 12) and fill with the corresponding message and Scripture (see chart on page 70). Open one egg each day, starting 12 days before Easter. Read the message aloud to the family and look up the Scripture in the Bible. Pray together, thanking the Lord for that particular aspect of the crucifixion and resurrection. (See next page.)

9. Plan and serve an Easter brunch and invite family, friends, and neighbors.

| Message (Front) | Scripture (Back) | Items |
|---|---|---|
| 1—Jesus rode into Jerusalem on a donkey. The people waved palm branches. | Matthew 21:1-11 | Piece of palm branch |
| 2—Mary poured expensive perfume on Jesus' head. | John 12:2-8 | Small perfume sample or cloth with perfume |
| 3—Jesus shared the Last Supper with His disciples. | Matthew 26:17-19 | Chex cereal |
| 4—Judas betrayed Jesus for 30 pieces of silver. | Matthew 27:3 | 3 dimes |
| 5—Jesus carried His own cross. | John 19:17 | Popsicle stick cut and glued in a cross form |
| 6—Soldiers placed a crown of thorns on Jesus' head. | John 19:2 | Small thorny branch |
| 7—Soldiers parted Jesus' garments and cast lots for His coat. | John 19:23 | Swatch of burlap and a nail |
| 8—Jesus was nailed to a cross and pierced in His side. | John 19:18,37; John 20:25-29 | A nail |
| 9—They gave Jesus vinegar mixed with gall on a sponge to drink. | Matthew 27:34 | A small sponge |
| 10—Spices to prepare Jesus for burial. | John 19:40 | 7 or 8 whole cloves |
| 11—The stone covering Jesus' tomb was rolled away. | John 20:1 | A small rock |
| 12—The napkin around Jesus' head was lying separately from His linen clothes. He was not there. He has risen! | John 20:6,7 | A scrap of linen-type fabric |

◆ Decorations or setting the mood—Place Easter lilies, baskets of tulips, wooden crosses, or spring bouquets around the house. Concentrate on the symbols of the Christian Easter.

◆ Table setting and centerpiece—Use a pink tablecloth with a white or ecru lace cover, allowing the pink to show through. If a lace cover is unavailable, white or ecru place mats can be used with contrasting pastel-colored napkins. Lay a spring flower across each napkin, or encircle it with a flower ring. At each place setting put a silver or white porcelain eggcup filled with a pastel-colored candle to be lit at the beginning of the meal. For a centerpiece, set an oblong mirror in the center of the table. Place a silver candelabra or silver candlesticks with tall pink or other pastel-colored candles on the mirror. At the base of the candlesticks arrange fresh-cut spring flowers or rings of fresh flowers. Set at each end of the mirror a figurine of Christian orientation (see your local Christian bookstore for ideas and selections).

---

**Easter Brunch**

*Ruby Breakfast Juice* or *Orange Juice*

*Turkey Sausage*

*Oven-Baked Spinach Mushroom Frittata*

*Tangerine Flowers* or *Mixed Fruit Bowl*

*Jam-Filled Scones*

*Strawberry Coconut Surprise Muffins*

*Herb Tea*

---

## ∞ Ruby Red Breakfast Juice

A tasty alternative to orange juice! If the specific brands given in this recipe cannot be located, look for other brands in supermarkets and health-food stores with similar quality of ingredients (as listed in the note below).

*Amount:* As desired (allow 1 cup or 8 ounces per serving)

*Chill and blend together:*

2 parts Smuckers Cranberry Juice
1 part Nice 'n Natural Ambrosia Fruit Juice Blend or Hansen's Natural Pineapple-Coconut Juice

Note: These juices are available in many supermarkets. Smuckers Cranberry Juice is made with white grape juice, cranberry juice concentrate, apple juice concentrate, and no sugar. Nice 'n Natural Ambrosia Fruit Juice Blend contains pineapple, orange, and coconut juices with no refined sugars added. No refined sugars are added to Hansen's Pineapple-Coconut Juice.

## ∞ Orange Juice

If you have access to an economical supply of fresh oranges, make quick work of juicing them with an electric juice squeezer. Plan on the following:

5 pounds oranges per 6 servings (approximately 8 ounces each)
(1 4.5-ounce medium orange yields about ⅓ cup juice)

If juice is squeezed in advance, cover tightly and store in a dark container in the refrigerator to minimize vitamin C loss.

To prepare frozen orange juice concentrate, plan on the following amount:

One 12-ounce can orange juice concentrate per 6 servings
(1 12-ounce can yields 48 ounces—6 8-ounce glasses)

## ∞ Turkey Sausage

A tasty alternative to bacon and pork sausage, ground turkey sausage contains ¼ the fat of pork sausage and less than ½ the calories, and ¹/₅ the fat of bacon with less than ¹/₃ the calories. Many guests cannot believe they are eating turkey when they are served this recipe!

*Amount:* 12 patties (serves 6)

1. Mix together thoroughly with a fork:

> 1 pound ground turkey
> 1 teaspoon salt
> ½ teaspoon nutmeg
> ½ teaspoon sage
> ½ teaspoon thyme
> ¹/₈ teaspoon cayenne pepper

2. Shape into 12 small patties. Fry in ungreased skillet or bake at 350° for 10 to 15 minutes in shallow pan until done. Do not overcook or patties will become tough. Oven baking produces juicier patties and is easier when feeding a crowd.

## ∞ *Oven-Baked Spinach Mushroom Frittata*

We have turned our Spinach Mushroom Omelette for two into a baked frittata that is easy to make for a crowd. There's no flipping or turning of eggs—just blend all and bake.

*Amount:* 6 to 8 servings

1. Steam, drain, and chop spinach; sauté onions and mushrooms in butter until barely tender:

> 1 head spinach
> 2 tablespoons melted butter
> 1 cup sliced fresh mushrooms
> 2 green onions, chopped

2. Combine remaining ingredients in order given. Stir in the vegetables and pour into well-buttered 9" x 13" pan:

    6 large eggs, beaten
    6 tablespoons water or milk
    ¼ teaspoon salt
    8 ounces cream cheese, crumbled into small pieces

3. Bake at 350° for 35 minutes or until a knife comes clean out of center. Serve as desired with avocado wedges, salsa.

## ∽ *Tangerine Flowers*

Plan for a colorful fruit garnish on the holiday brunch plate. If the tangerine season has not quite extended into early spring, try this garnish idea as a springboard for your imagination and use another fruit.

1. Score skins of tangerines with sharp knife into six equal wedges around outside of tangerines.

2. Peel the skin petals back ⅔ of the way, leaving intact at the base of tangerines.

3. Carefully loosen center of tangerine and separate sections inside the skin, leaving them intact at the base. Fan them out slightly.

4. Garnish center of tangerine with 1 or 2 slices of kiwi, a parsley sprig, mint leaf, or tangerine leaf.

## ∽ *Mixed Fruit Bowl*

Serve a bowl of two, three, or more fresh fruits to go on top of waffles or alongside them. The following are some of our favorite combinations, but only the season need limit your selection. A single fresh fruit, chopped or sliced, is also delicious. You can also top the fruit with whipped cream.

*Amount:* Allow ½ cup per serving

    strawberries, peaches, blueberries
    peaches, pineapple

nectarines, pineapple
nectarines, blueberries
peaches, blackberries

If desired sprinkle fruit lightly with crystalline fructose or sugar.

## ∞ Whipped Cream

*Amount:* 2 cups (serves 6, ⅓ cup each)

1. In electric mixer on high speed whip for about 30 seconds:

    ½ pint whipping or heavy cream

2. Add gradually, continuing to whip until thickened:

    2 tablespoons mild-flavored honey or crystalline fructose (health-food store)

## ∞ Jam-Filled Scones

Easy-to-make, yummy-to-eat tender morsels! Bake before the frittata.

*Amount:* 12 to 15 scones (serves 6)

1. Blend together:

    2 cups whole-wheat pastry flour (health-food store)
    ¼ cup crystalline fructose (health-food store)
    ½ teaspoon cinnamon
    ½ teaspoon baking power (low-sodium baking powder from health-food store preferred)
    ½ teaspoon baking soda
    ½ teaspoon salt

2. With two table knives or a pastry blender cut butter into dry ingredients until size of small peas:

    ¼ cup butter

3. Blend in to make a firm dough; knead 8 strokes:

   ⅔ cup buttermilk

4. Pat dough to ¾" thick. Dip a 2" cookie cutter or rim of glass in flour and cut 2" biscuits out of the dough.

5. Place biscuits on ungreased cookie sheet and let stand 10 minutes; brush with cream or egg yolk for a shiny surface, if desired.

6. Bake at 400° for 12 to 15 minutes.

7. Heat in microwave for about 1 minute:

   ½ cup jam or preserves

8. Gently slice baked scones in half. Spread bottom halves with about 1½ teaspoons jam; top with other halves and serve.

## ⊗ Strawberry Coconut Surprise Muffins

A delightful breakfast, dessert, or snack muffin. Best served warm.

*Amount:* 10 medium muffins

1. Spray muffin pan with no-stick cooking spray (Olive Oil Pam Spray preferred).

2. Blend together and let stand for 30 minutes:

   1 cup buttermilk
   1 cup uncooked rolled oats

3. Blend thoroughly into oat mixture:

   1 egg
   ¼ cup honey or crystalline fructose (health-food store)
   ¾ cup shredded coconut, unsweetened (health-food store)

4. Blend dry ingredients together in separate bowl:

   1 cup whole wheat pastry flour (health-food store)

1½ teaspoons baking powder (low-sodium baking powder from
   health-food store preferred)
½ teaspoon baking soda
½ teaspoon salt

5. Blend dry ingredients into liquid ingredients just until mixed.
   Do not overmix.

6. Fill muffin cups about half full. Place in center of each:

   1 scant teaspoon strawberry preserves

7. Cover preserves on each muffin with dab of remaining dough.

8. Bake at 400° for 20 minutes. Cool 2 minutes or longer (until
   muffins come out of pan easily).

## ∞ *Herb Tea*

With the rich flavors of the menu, serve complementary mild
hot drinks of regular and decaffeinated coffee, and spiced herb teas.
Purchase 3 or 4 choices of herb teas that are individually packaged
in colorful wrappers. Put a pot of piping-hot water on the table
with a tray or bowl of herb tea bags, allowing guests to choose and
prepare their own. Provide honey, cream, and lemon wedges.

## Family Sunrise Service

### *Ahead of Time*

   ✦ Choose a special, quiet place from which the sunrise can
     be seen.

   ✦ Prepare a simple carry-along breakfast of boiled eggs, rolls,
     juice, etc. (If you like, each person's breakfast could be
     packed in a colorful Easter basket. Surprises could be hid-
     den in the bottom of each basket.)

✦ Find and mark the Easter story in the Bible.

✦ Choose one or two songs the whole family can sing about the risen Lord, or take along a cassette player and taped music the family can sing along with.

✦ The week before Easter, read from a Bible story book or from the Bible the events leading up to the resurrection (Matthew 26 and 27) and discuss them.

✦ The night before Easter, talk about how the disciples must have felt on the Saturday night before the resurrection; how Jesus' mother must have felt; what Mary Magdalene and those who had known Jesus were feeling.

---

*Our children are like jewels, to be polished by us and given to the Lord.*

---

## Easter Morning

✦ Rise early enough to give the family time to get to your special place just before the sun comes up.

✦ Wear clothes that can be gotten into quickly (you can get ready for church later). Take warm jackets and blankets.

✦ Spread a blanket to sit on, then read together about the women going to Jesus' tomb and what they experienced.

✦ As the sun comes peeping over the horizon, sing or play a victorious song. Then thank God with your eyes wide open for the resurrection and what it means to your family.

✦ Celebrate by sharing the simple breakfast you have brought with you.

# Symbols of Easter

Many times we enjoy the symbols of a special day without really understanding their significance. Easter symbols are especially rich in meaning. Before Easter, discuss as a family the meanings of these symbols we so much enjoy.

+ *Spring*. Easter and spring belong together. What a wonderful time to celebrate newness of life and the resurrection when all nature is "rising again."

+ *Baby bunnies, chicks, birds*. All newly born creatures remind us of the new birth we have in Christ. Because of Easter, we can become "new creatures" in Him.

+ *The green, yellow, pink, and lavender colors of springtime*. These are perfect symbols of Easter. The earth bursts forth into color with the proclamation, "Life wins!" Green also stands for new life, and lavender, the color of royalty, reminds us that Jesus is King of kings and Lord of lords.

+ *New clothes*. A new outfit symbolizes the putting away of winter—the time when it seems all nature hides "in the tomb"—and the dressing up of the earth in the lovely new clothes of spring. We, too, because of Christ bursting from the tomb, are "clothed in newness of life."

+ *Eggs*. Eggs, of course, are the epitome of promised life— life sealed away for a time before new life literally bursts forth! Eggs also symbolize in Jewish tradition a freewill offering—the giving of more than is demanded. Jesus is God's freewill offering. God gives us far beyond what we deserve or even dare to ask. Jesus is the gift not only of life, but of eternal life.[2]

## "Jesus Is Risen"

Try writing messages on the eggs with crayons before dyeing as a reminder of the real meaning of Easter. Examples of messages are:

- ✦ Jesus Is Love
- ✦ Jesus Loves You
- ✦ Praise God
- ✦ Love—Forever
- ✦ Jesus Died for You
- ✦ Born Again
- ✦ He Is Risen
- ✦ For God So Loved the World
- ✦ Love Changes Things
- ✦ Hallelujah
- ✦ Lord of Lords

Climax the day and evening by renting one of the great classic Easter films on video. Check with your local video rental store on availability.

## Easter Sunday Night Dinner

One of my dearest young lady friends, Marita Littauer Noon, describes in her book *Homemade Memories* a wonderful Easter Sunday dinner.[3] She shares recipes that her family has used for many years. Her menu is as follows:

---

**Traditional Easter Sunday Dinner**

*Easter Ham (or Turkey or Roast Beef)*

*Candied Carrots*

*Rice Pilaf*

*Lemon Meringue Pie*

---

Marita includes a ham recipe her mother made regularly for Easter and other occasions. It is a basic ham studded with cloves and basted throughout the cooking time with a brown sugar and mustard glaze. With this dinner, a vegetable with a sweet touch is appropriate. The candied carrots come from her grandmother's collection of fine recipes. They are sweet, fresh, and give a nice color to the Easter dinner plate. With the glazed ham and candied carrots, the starch should be light, so a buttery rice pilaf fits the meal perfectly. To top off this colorful menu, Marita suggests lemon meringue pie (one of my Bob's favorites). The yellow color fits in with the Easter scheme, and the fluffy meringue adds to the lightness of the meal.

This is a meal you will want more often than once a year. Since everything involved in making this festive feast is available all year long, why wait for Easter? Celebrate our risen Lord anytime. Christ is risen, indeed!

## Timetable

*3 hours before serving:*

> Score the ham.
> Prepare the glaze.

*2½ hours before serving:*

> Place ham in the oven.
> Prepare the Lemon Meringue Pie.

*2 hours before serving:*

> Take a rest!

*35 minutes before serving:*

> Prepare the Rice Pilaf.

*15 minutes before serving:*

> Prepare the carrots.

## Shopping List

### Stock Items

| | |
|---|---|
| brown sugar | sugar |
| cornstarch | dried parsley flakes |
| dried minced onion flakes | salt |
| pepper | chicken bouillon cubes |
| eggs | butter |
| bacon fat | prepared mustard |

### Special purchases

½ ham, butt portion
12 medium carrots
3 lemons
vermicelli
white rice (Blue Rose type)
one 9-inch piecrust

## ⊗ Easter Ham (optional)

*Preheat oven to 325°.*

½ fully cooked ham, butt portion (usually 6–8 pounds)
whole cloves
½ cup brown sugar
½ cup prepared mustard
3 tablespoons melted bacon fat

Score the fatty portion of the ham to create a diamond-shaped pattern with the diamonds about 1 inch across. Place a clove, pointed side down, into the fat of each diamond shape. Place the ham, fat side facing up, in a roasting pan.

In a small bowl combine the brown sugar, mustard, and bacon fat. Brush the ham with the glaze, coating the fat and the meaty sides lightly with glaze. (There will be quite a bit of glaze left.) Place the ham in the oven and cook 2 to 2½ hours. Brush the ham with more glaze every half hour or until there is no more glaze.

If you are serving a larger crowd and are using a whole ham, score the fatty covering just as for the half ham, double the glaze, and cook 12 to 15 minutes per pound.

## ∞ Candied Carrots

    12 medium carrots
    2 tablespoons butter
    2 tablespoons brown sugar

Trim and peel or clean the carrots. Slice them into ⅓-inch-thick slices and place the sliced carrots in the top portion of a microwave vegetable steamer. Place a couple of tablespoons of water in the bottom of the steamer, add the top portion, and cover. Cook on high in the microwave for 8 minutes or until carrots reach the desired tenderness. Pour the water out of the bottom portion. Empty the cooked carrots into the bottom portion. Add the butter and brown sugar. Replace the cover and shake the steamer until the carrots are fully covered with the butter and brown sugar. Serve.

## ∞ Rice Pilaf

An Armenian friend from Fresno, California, first introduced me to rice pilaf. I loved it so much I asked her to show me how to make it. I have since lost her real recipe, but I think she would be happy with my adaptation.

    8 tablespoons butter
    2 coils of dry, uncooked vermicelli (a fine, spaghetti-like pasta
        that comes in a coil which slightly resembles a bird's nest.
        There are several coils per package.)
    2 cups white rice (not the quick-cooking kind)
    4 cups water
    2 chicken bouillon cubes

1 tablespoon dried parsley
1 tablespoon minced onion flakes
1 teaspoon salt
freshly ground pepper

Using a large saucepan, melt the butter over medium heat. Break the coils of vermicelli into little pieces and add them to the melted butter. Cook until the vermicelli has a nice golden color, stirring frequently (about 5 minutes). Add the rice and stir until the rice is nicely coated with butter (about 2 minutes). Add the remaining ingredients and stir to blend. Reduce the heat to low. Cover the pan and cook over low heat until all the liquid is absorbed (about 25 minutes). Stir a couple of times throughout the cooking process. Fluff the rice with a fork before serving.

## ∽ Lemon Meringue Pie

*Amount:* one 8-slice pie

*Preheat oven to 350°*

*Filling:*

1½ cups sugar
7 tablespoons cornstarch
a dash of salt
1½ cups water
3 beaten egg yolks
grated peel of 1 lemon
2 tablespoons butter
½ cup lemon juice

Using a medium saucepan, combine the sugar, cornstarch, and salt. Stir well, to the point that the cornstarch is completely mixed in with the sugar. Stir in the water. Bring the mixture to a boil over medium heat and cook until the mixture thickens and is translucent, stirring continuously.

Remove the pan from the heat and stir a small amount (about 1 tablespoon) of the sugar mixture into the egg yolks. Pour all of the egg-yolk mixture into the sugar mixture. Return the pan to the heat and bring to a boil, stirring continuously. Once the mixture comes to a boil, remove it from the heat. Stir in the butter. Once the butter has melted and blended, stir in the lemon peel. Set the mixture aside to cool. Stir it occasionally to prevent a film from forming on the top.

*Meringue:*

4 egg whites
1 teaspoon lemon juice
6 tablespoons sugar

Using an electric mixer, beat the egg whites and the lemon juice together until soft peaks form. Continue beating and add the sugar, 1 tablespoon at a time, until all the sugar has dissolved and the egg whites form stiff peaks.

Pour the lemon filling into the piecrust. Top the filling with the egg-white mixture. Spread the egg whites to the edge of the pastry. Using a spoon, create peaks and valleys in the meringue.

Bake 12 to 15 minutes at 350° or until the meringue is golden brown. (If you are cooking the pie at the same time as the ham, turn up the oven temperature for the 15 minutes needed to brown the meringue, then return it to 325°.) Allow the pie to cool before serving. Cut into 8 pieces and serve.

## ⌐ Marita's Piecrust

*Amount:* 2 single piecrusts

2 cups regular flour (I use unbleached, although any regular flour will work fine.)
1 teaspoon salt
¾ cup Butter Flavor Crisco (use only Butter Flavor Crisco— very important)
¼ cup water

In a large bowl, combine the flour and salt. Using a pastry blender, mix in the Butter Flavor Crisco until the particles are pea-sized and the mixture looks like coarse oatmeal. Sprinkle the mixture with the water and toss with a fork to combine. Using your hands, reach into the bowl and press the mixture into a ball.

Don't worry if there are little bits that don't mix in. Be careful to handle the dough as little as possible. It is not like bread dough where you must knead it frequently—overhandling makes a pie-crust tough.

Use a pastry cloth on the counter and a pastry sleeve on the rolling pin. These are important items for a perfect crust. Sprinkle flour on the pastry cloth and roll the rolling pin in the flour to coat the pastry sleeve.

Once the dough is in a ball, break the ball in half and shape it into another ball. On the pastry cloth, press the ball down until it looks like a thick pancake. Roll the dough with strokes from the center out using the rolling pin. Once the dough is at least 1 inch larger than the edge of the pie plate, stop rolling. Place the pie plate on top of the dough, facedown. Cut the edge of the dough about 2 fingers' width from the edge of the pie plate. Remove the edge pieces. Leave the pie plate on the dough and fold the edges of the pastry cloth over the pie plate. With your hand, reach under the pastry cloth so your hand is in the center of the crust and flip the whole thing over. Peel off the pastry cloth.

Your crust should now be perfectly centered on the pie plate. If it is not, adjust it. Fold under the edges that are hanging over the rim of the pie plate; crimp them to make a pretty edge. To crimp, lightly pinch the edge with both hands. With one thumb and forefinger press the dough inward and with the other thumb and forefinger press out. Continue this technique all around the crust.

Repeat the previous steps for the second crust.

If you are only using one crust, wrap the other tightly in plastic wrap or place in a large zippered storage bag and freeze. The crust will last nicely for several weeks. To bake an empty piecrust, prick it all over with a fork and bake it in a 425° oven 10 to 15 minutes, until golden brown. (Do not bake the crust first if you are using it for an apple pie.)

# Kids' Helps

*Easter Ham:* Older children can stick the cloves into the diamond-pattern cuts you have made in the ham. A younger child can mix the ingredients for the glaze and brush the ham with the glaze before it goes into the oven.

*Candied Carrots:* Once the carrots are cooked, a child can shake the microwave steamer to coat the carrots with the sugar and butter.

*Rice Pilaf:* Have a child stir the vermicelli until it is lightly browned. Add the rice and have the child continue stirring while you add the remaining ingredients.

*Lemon Meringue Pie:* Once all the dry ingredients are in the saucepan, let a child stir them until they are fully blended. Let the child continue stirring while you add the water and the mixture cooks. After you have mixed a small amount of the sugar mixture into the egg yolks, let the child stir while you pour all of the egg yolks into the saucepan and continue to stir while the mixture comes to a boil.

This recipe involves a lot of stirring, so several children may need to take turns. They are apt to need lots of encouragement at this point. Let them drop in the butter pieces while you stir the mixture to blend in the butter.

For the meringue, once you have separated the eggs, let the children take turns beating the egg whites using the electric beater. Once the egg whites have formed soft peaks, add the sugar and continue to beat the egg whites to form stiff peaks.[3]

# 5

## Mother's Day

"HONOR YOUR FATHER AND YOUR MOTHER, that your days may be prolonged in the land which the LORD your God gives you" (Exodus 20:12).

**When Observed:** Second Sunday in May

**Earliest Observance in United States:** May 10, 1908; Grafton, West Virginia

The honoring of mothers can be traced back centuries before the birth of Christ. But today's second-Sunday-in-May holiday, commercialized with candy and carnations, was conceived in America.

The ancient mother goddess Cybele had been the center of an ancient Greek cult continued by the Romans as the festival of Hilaria. Later, as Christianity spread, the early church fathers developed ceremonies for the veneration of the Virgin Mary, as well as reverence for the "Mother Church."

In England on the fourth Sunday of Lent, people might visit the "Mother Church" of their baptism. Later, young men and women, working as apprentices and servants, would be given Mid-Lent (or "Mothering") Sunday to bring to their mothers a kind of rich fruit cake (similia). More recently, children in the East End of London would bring nosegays (small bouquets) of violets and primroses to their mothers on Mothering Sunday, after getting the flowers blessed at church.

Amazingly, in Yugoslavia, on one Sunday in December the children will *tie up* Mother till she promises to provide sweets and goodies. (The week before this the parents tie up the children till they promise to be good; the Sunday after the children tie up mother is Dad's turn. A quaint prelude to Christmas . . . )

The first Mother's Day observance was a church service held in Grafton, West Virginia, on May 10, 1908, to honor motherhood and pay homage to Mrs. Anna Reese Jarvis. Her daughter, Anna M. Jarvis, was instrumental in establishing this day to honor mothers in general, but also to honor her own mother.

The carnation, which has become so traditional and familiar on Mother's Day, was part of this first service. This was one of Mrs. Jarvis's favorite flowers.

By 1911 every state in the Union had adopted its own day for the observance of Mother's Day. On May 9, 1914, a resolution providing that the second Sunday in May be designated Mother's Day was issued by President Woodrow Wilson.

Today, Mother's Day is a popular occasion, warm and joyful in spirit. Flowers and gifts are often the order of the day. Greetings are designed to be sent not only to one's own mother but also to grandmothers, aunts, mothers of wives and sweethearts, and to anyone who merits the accolades of motherhood.

---

*You are the mother I received the day I wed your son; and I just want to thank you, Mom, for all the things you've done. You've given me a gracious man with whom I share my life; you are his lovely mother, and I his thankful wife*—A Thankful Wife.

---

When I think of motherhood, I'm reminded of one great mother of the eighteenth century, Sarah Edwards, whose vital interest in her children's development had a lasting impact. Married to the famous clergyman and theologian Jonathan Edwards, she was the mother of 11 children. At the same time, Sarah maintained a vital and intensely loving marriage.

Writing about the Edwards family, author Elizabeth Dodds says straightforwardly, "The way children turn out is always a reflection on their mother."

Dodds refers to a study done by A.E. Winship in 1900 in which he lists some of the accomplishments of the 1400 Edwards family descendants he located. The Edwards family produced:

    13 college presidents
    65 professors
    100 lawyers and a dean of a law school
    30 judges
    66 physicians and a dean of a medical school
    80 holders of public office
    3 United States senators
    3 state governors
    1 vice president of the United States
    1 controller of the United States Treasury

Winship believed that "much of the capacity and talent, intensity and character of the more than 1,400 of the Edwards family is due to Mrs. Edwards."

How did Sarah Edwards do it? A deeply devout Christian woman, Sarah emerges from the pages of Dodds's book as a firm, patient mother who treated her children with courtesy and love. Samuel Hopkins, a contemporary who spent time in the Edwards', household, said Sarah was able to guide her children without angry words or blows. Unlike many mothers today, Sarah had only to speak once and her children obeyed her.

"In their manners they were uncommonly respectful to their parents. When their parents came into the room, they all rose instinctively from their seats and never resumed them until their parents were seated." These children who were so well-treated by their parents in turn loved and respected them as well as each other.

*Who ran to help me when I fell,*
*And would some pretty story tell,*
*Or kiss the place to make it well?*
*My mother*—Jane Taylor.

In the management of her busy colonial home, Sarah puts her modern counterparts to shame. We, who have only to press a button to start our many machines, can hardly imagine the sheer physical labor required of the colonial housewife. Sarah had many hard tasks: to see that the candles and clothes were made, the food prepared, the garden planted, the fire stoked, and guests fed and comfortably housed. Contiguously, she taught her children to work and deal with life.

Dodds also portrays Sarah as a keen observer of human nature:

> [She] carefully observed the first appearance of resentment and ill will in her young children, toward any person, whatever, and did not connive at it ... but was careful to show her displeasure and suppress it to the utmost; yet not by angry, wrathful words, which often provoke children to wrath. ... Her system of discipline was begun at a very early age and it was her rule to resist the first, as well as every subsequent exhibition of temper or disobedience in the child ... wisely reflecting that until a child will obey his parents, he will never be brought to obey God.

As a disciplinarian, Sarah clearly defined her boundaries and tolerated no misbehavior from her children. The result was a household that emanated love and harmony.

As Elizabeth Dodds makes abundantly clear in her book, a mother is not merely rearing her one generation of children. She is also affecting future generations for good or ill. All the love, nurture, education, and character-building that spring from Mother's work influence those sons and daughters. The results show up in the children's accomplishments, attitudes toward life, and parenting capacity. For example, one of Sarah Edwards's grandsons, Timothy Dwight, president of Yale (echoing Lincoln), said, "All that I am and all that I shall be, I owe to my mother."

As one ponders this praise, the question arises: Are we women unhappy in our mothering role because we make too little, rather than too much, of that role? Do we see what we have to give our children as minor rather than major, and consequently send them into the world without a healthy core identity and strong spiritual values?

---

*Women like to make sacrifices in one
big piece, to give God something grand.
    But we can't.
Our lives are a mosaic of
    little things, like putting
    a rose in a vase on the table.
Sometimes we don't see how much
    those things mean.*
    —Ingrid Trobisch

---

It was the great investment of time that mothers like Sarah Edwards and Susanna Wesley made in the lives of their children that garnered each such high praise. One can't teach a child to read in an hour or stretch a child's mind in a few days.

Have we as mothers unwisely left our children's education to school and church, believing that we can fill in around the edges? And would we feel better about ourselves if we were more actively involved in teaching our children? I think so.

A thread runs throughout the whole of life: Only as we invest much will the yield be great. Our children are growing up in a rough, tough world, and they need us to invest a lot of time and energy in their lives. Only then will they—and we—experience significant gain.[1]

Wow! What a mother! I could feel guilty if I compared myself to Sarah Edwards. But I know this: I did the best I knew how to do. Perfect mom? No, not by a long shot. I learned a lot along the way, and I'm still learning. Being open to God's Word and His promises are all the tools I need to be the mother into which God is molding me.

---

*God made woman from man's rib—not from his head to top him, nor from his feet to be walked upon, but from his side to be his partner in life, from under his arm to be protected by him, and near his heart to be loved by him.*

---

The following acrostic is what *Mother* means to me:

## M ∞ *Makes Time for Daily Prayer to God*

Matthew 6:33 (KJV) says, "Seek ye first the kingdom of God, and his righteousness; and all these things shall be added unto you." This verse establishes my first priority as a mother: setting aside time each day for prayer.

The prayer basket I made for myself contains my Bible, a pen, a box of tissue, stationery, a few silk flowers in a small jar, and my prayer notebook.

My prayer notebook is a three-ring binder with prayer request sheets, tabs labeled Monday through Sunday, and sheets for sermon notes. (See sample at end of chapter.)

I organized this to give me "more hours in my day" while also spending quality time with my Lord and praying for all the needs of family and friends.

For each day of the week, I've delegated several topics for which to pray. (See sample topic page at end of chapter.) Example:

*Monday*—home organization, family. I have a page for each immediate member of the family—Bob, Brad, Craig, Jenny, etc. For each grandchild, I've drawn their handprint on a page and made a heart in the middle. On Monday when I pray for them, I place my hand on theirs, and our hearts beat together as I give the Lord my requests. *Tuesday*—illnesses (my Auntie Phyllis who broke her hip; Brooke, who has M.S.). *Wednesday*—our church pastor and staff people. *Thursday*—self, personal finances. *Friday*—our country, city, state, president. *Saturday*—missionaries at home and abroad. *Sunday*—sermon notes (this is where I record and outline the sermon and any church prayer requests. Later, these requests can be integrated into the proper tab section. Scriptures can be recorded for future reference. See end of chapter for sample page).

My prayer basket goes with me wherever I spend time in prayer: in the backyard under a tree in the summer; by a lake or stream; by the fireplace in the winter with a cup of tea; in an office, bedroom, or perhaps in the bathroom where I know I can be alone. My prayer basket has all the tools I need to "seek first the kingdom of God."

## O ∽ Open to the Lord

I want to have a heart like Jesus. Psalm 139 (NIV) says it all:

> O LORD, you have searched me
> and you know me.
> You know when I sit and when I rise;
> you perceive my thoughts from afar.
> You discern my going out and my lying down;
> you are familiar with all my ways.
> Before a word is on my tongue
> you know it completely, O LORD.
>
> You hem me in—behind and before;
> you have laid your hand upon me.

Such knowledge is too wonderful for me,
 too lofty for me to attain. . . .
For you created my inmost being;
 you knit me together in my mother's womb.
I praise you because I am fearfully
  and wonderfully made;
 your works are wonderful,
 I know that full well.
My frame was not hidden from you
 when I was made in the secret place.
When I was woven together in the depths of the earth,
 your eyes saw my unformed body.
All the days ordained for me
 were written in your book
 before one of them came to be. . . .
Search me, O God, and know my heart;
 test me and know my anxious thoughts.
See if there is any offensive way in me,
 and lead me in the way everlasting.

After reading this passage of Scripture, I am amazed that God knows me so intimately. He alone is familiar with all my characteristics, which have become a part of me through my parents and grandparents.

He knows and understands my personality and human behavior more than anyone else. He is fair and just to me. Since He has known me from conception, He knows what's best for me (even when I refuse to listen to God's words).

Through this love He never rejects or despises me. Instead, He begins to create in me a new heart, like His own loving likeness. Through this change of heart, He works on my mind, emotions, and behavior. God understands why I think and feel as I do from day to day as I interface with others around me.

In all these complex activities, He does not condemn me; instead, He comes to change and redirect my values, pride, decisions, thoughts, purpose, and service.

Because of this knowing of me, I want to be open to Him on this very special Mother's Day. I recommit this day to Him and I want to be open to everything He has for me as a wife, mother, and woman.

## T ∞ Trusts in the Lord

Our hope as mothers is found through spending time with our Bibles to study God's Word. If you aren't already in the habit of having daily devotions with your Lord, why not begin today? Go to your local Christian bookstore and request help in finding just the right devotional for you. It takes 21 days to begin a new habit. Try this for these next 21 days, and you will be amazed at what new zeal you have for life. Set your alarm 10 to 15 minutes earlier each morning. Rise, read, and shine. Trust God to perform a new work in you.

## H ∞ Has Healing in Relationships Through Christ

A mother seeks forgiveness in relationships so that a healing process can take place. If mother and daughter or mother and son have out-of-order relationships, these must be brought to the surface and bathed in prayer for a complete cleansing.

When my mother went home to be with the Lord at 78 years of age, she left me with two very beautiful gifts: her belief in the Messiah and the knowledge that one day we will be in glory together, and the memory of all the loving times of sweet fellowship we had together.

Guilt feelings can eat you up inside—so clean out the wounds and pour the healing ointment of love and forgiveness inside.

## E ∞ Enriched by the Lord

Teach us, O Lord, as mothers, so we can teach others. Titus 2:4

says that the older women are to teach the younger women to love their husbands and to be makers of a home. That's what Sarah Edwards did as a mother. As mothers, we can take life experiences and teach them to others and, through it all, we, too, will learn.

Think of someone today whom you can disciple. It might be a son, daughter, a sister, a neighbor, or someone at work. There is always someone you know who knows less about Jesus than you do. Open your eyes and ears and become aware of those all around you who need their lives enriched. Reach out and touch them.

## R ∽ Reaches up to God

I'm choosing to make God the Lord of my life. This is the best choice I can make; it gives me a purpose and a peace during the tough times.

Let's exchange our earthly desires for heavenly desires. We'll be more alive in death than in life when we do, and our beautiful years of motherhood will never really end if our hearts can daily reach up to God in love and prayer.

I received this letter from our son, Brad, one year on Mother's Day when he was away at college. It is the best gift I ever received from him, and yet it cost only his time.

*Thank You, God,*

*For pretending not to notice that one of Your angels is missing and for guiding her to me. You must have known how much I would need her, so You turned Your head for a minute and allowed her to slip away to me. Sometimes I wonder what special name You had for her. I call her "Mother."*

*To think of not having her with me is unbearable. I don't know what I would have done without her all these years. She has loved me without reservation—whether I deserved to be loved or not. Willingly and happily, she has fed me, clothed me, taught me, encouraged me, inspired me, and with her own special brand of gentleness reprimanded me. A bit of heaven's own blue, her eyes reflect hope and love for You and her family. She has tried to instill that love in us.*

*She's not the least bit afraid of work. With her constant scrubbing, polishing, painting, and fixing she has made every house we've lived in, a beautiful home. When I'm confused, she sets me straight. She knows what matters and what doesn't. What to hold on to and what to let go. You have given her an endless supply of love. She gives it away freely yet never seems to run low. Even before I am aware I have a need, she is making plans and working to supply it. You gave her great patience. She is the best listener I have met. With understanding and determination she always seems to turn a calamity into some kind of success. She urges me to carry my own load in life but is always close by if I stumble under the burden. She hurts when I hurt. She cries when I cry. And she will not be happy until she has seen a smile on my face once more. Although she has taught me to pray, she has never ceased to invoke Your richest blessings upon me.*

*Thank the other angels for filling in for her while she is away. I know it hasn't been easy. Her shoes would be hard to fill. She has to be one of Your greatest miracles, God, and I want to thank You for lending my mother to me.*

You can imagine the tears I shed when I read this. Proverbs 31:28 flashed before me: "Her children arise and call her blessed." Again, God, You are so good when You give me confirmation that all of those endless days and nights of serving my family were recognized by my son, Brad.

These words of encouragement and thanksgiving were all that I needed on this day. Again I say, "It's worth it all, even when it seems like no one notices or cares."

## Gifts of Self

None of the following gift suggestions costs anything, yet each is one-of-a-kind and bound to please because it's a gift of yourself.

Every day should be a day in which we honor all members of our family, but this day should be extra-special for Mom. These may be the greatest gifts Mom will ever receive.

---

*What the heart gives away is never gone....It is kept in the hearts of others*—Robin St. John.

---

1. *The gift of a compliment*—Perhaps you could make a list of the qualities you admire in your mother: her sense of humor, her survival instinct, her ability to live without impossible expectations. You might praise her cooking, her patience, her intelligence, or her sensitivity.

2. *A gift of thanks*—It's strange how much we take from others and how little we return. A thank you is a simple act—not always expected and therefore very valuable. Thank Mom for having endured your childhood years that required her constant attention, for the thousands of meals she cooked, for the tons of laundry she did—and most important, for just being there.

3. *A gift of affection*—How about a warm embrace, a kiss on the cheek, a moment of hand-holding? All of us need affection no matter what our age or how much we protest that it's not our style.

4. *A gift of listening*—Everyone has known the frustration of wanting to be heard and finding that no one is interested in listening. One of the most valuable things we can do for each other is to be a good listener.

5. *The gift of a note*—Write your mother a personal note, unabashedly sentimental, full of loving thoughts—which may become her newest family treasure. If you find yourself lacking the right words, a simple "Mom, I love you" can say so much.

6. *A gift of forgiveness*—People are not perfect. Those closest to us often seem the least so. We owe them the same forgiveness we expect for our own imperfections. An act of forgiveness can start things anew and reunite us as nothing else can.

7. *A gift of laughter*—If so far none of these gifts interest you, try a gift of laughter. Nothing unites like laughter. Perhaps you can take Mom out for a day of doing all the crazy things she used to love—just a day for accumulating new, joyous memories between mother and daughter or son.

8. *A gift of time*—Make an appointment with Mom so that just the two of you can spend some time together. You don't need to plan any activity—just share time. Tell Mom how special she is to you.

9. *A gift of relaxation*—Tell Mom that she has the evening off. You're going to prepare supper, set the table, clean off the table, and wash the dishes. Mom can go read the paper or a good book, listen to music, watch television, or just take a nap. It's Mom's night off.

## Special Gifts

1. *Special treats*—If you still live at home with Mom, talk with Dad and plan some special activities for her. Really make a big deal out of this day.

   ◆ Treat Mom with breakfast in bed.

   ◆ A delightful gift if you are low on money is to give Mom a cute coupon stating that it is good for clearing off the dinner dishes for a week, doing the ironing for a week, or loading the dishwasher (or washing the dishes by hand) for a week.

   ◆ Plan a picnic for Mom.

   ◆ Use an oven mitt as the wrapping for a small gift.

   ◆ Take Mom to church and share with her how much you

appreciate her giving you Christian training. Include a big thank you for the prayers she shares with you each night, etc. After church you can go out for brunch (if you do, be sure to make reservations at least two weeks in advance) or prepare a brunch for her at home. Mom will love the special treatment.

2. *Long-distance appreciation*—If you no longer live at home, you still need to take time to honor Mom.

+ Take or send her flowers.

+ Take or send her a card.

+ If out of town, start early and give her a telephone call. (Since the telephone lines are extremely busy on Mother's Day, you might try to make that call the day before.)

+ If you are close enough to see her on this day, set up a time to be with her.

3. *A gift of perfume*—As a family, go to the local mall and purchase some wonderful fragrances, shampoos, and bath oils and put them in a cute basket. Wrap it with cello paper, tie a bow around the top of the wrap, and include a sweet note to Mom. Take the opportunity to make Mom feel very special on this, her day.

4. *Helping hands*—

+ Dad or the older children can trace Mother's hands on a folded piece of 8½" x 11" paper. Draw one hand on the front of the paper and one on the back; the inside of the folded paper will be used for a message.

+ Let the smaller children color the hand picture, drawing in Mother's watch, ring, fingernails, etc.

+ Help the children compose a note to put inside the paper that expresses appreciation for the loving things that are done by Mother: fixing dinner, ironing, putting on Band-

Aids, making repairs on the house, fixing toys, reading stories, etc.

+ At the bottom of the page write, "We appreciate you, Mom."

+ Give the card to Mom on Mother's Day.

5. *Family card*—

+ Fold a large sheet (12" x 18") of construction paper in half.

+ Decorate the front of the card with a greeting or picture. If Mom has a hobby, perhaps a picture related to that activity would be appropriate.

+ Glue a snapshot of each person in the family inside the card and have each person write a message of love under his/her picture. These messages might all begin with "You're special to me because..." or "One reason I love you so is..." or "I remember when you..."

6. *Promise coupons*—Make a coupon book for Mom filled with promises of helpful things you will do. These coupons may be used any time in the next year.

+ Cut blank index cards into equal coupon-size pieces.

+ On each card write, "This coupon good for..." and name one chore or favor:
> doing dinner dishes one time
> cleaning the garage
> raking leaves for one hour
> one car wash
> one hour of window-washing
> one hour of playing Scrabble (or other game of Mom's choice)
> one week of feeding the dog

+ Save one coupon piece to make an attractive cover for the coupon book.

♦ Staple all the coupons together and put the coupon book in an envelope.

♦ Tie a ribbon around the envelope and lay it on Mom's plate before dinner or breakfast.[2]

In many homes, Mother's Day can become most traumatic. Usually the family members want to do something special for Mom, so they try to cook a special breakfast or take Mom out to a restaurant. Many dads are unfamiliar with the kitchen and food preparation, and it can become a disaster where Mom has to intervene and even clean up after her own breakfast.

---

*Keep your ideals high enough to inspire you, and low enough to encourage you.*

---

A trip to a restaurant can be even worse. The wait can be long, the meal hurried, and the service lacking. Many years ago, we as a family said, "No more going out to restaurants on Mother's Day. Let's find a meal that Dad and the children can make—a no-loser menu."

With the help of Sue Gregg and Marita Littauer, I include in this chapter two such menus found in Marita's book *Homemade Memories*.

The first menu features a single surprise breakfast that can be prepared before church, and the second menu includes a lovely dinner for later in the day.

To start out, Dad needs to review the shopping list for both menus to see which items are already in the house and which ones he will need to purchase before Mother's Day.

On the big day, Dad and the children need to get up an hour early. Encourage Mom to stay in bed and get some extra rest, read the Sunday newspaper, and have a cup of fresh-brewed tea or coffee.

Have the children set the table with the prettiest dishes. Cut a few fresh flowers or sprigs of ivy, light some candles, spray a little fragrance in the air, and call Mom to the table when all is ready (serving Mom her breakfast would be fine, too).

Follow the complete timetable for preparing the breakfast, or after church begin preparation of the dinner. If you follow the timetable and directions closely, Mom and the family will have a stress-free Mother's Day.

---

**Mother's Day Breakfast**

*Freshly Squeezed*
*Orange Juice*

*Turkey Sausages*

*Homemade Apple Pancakes*

Serves 4

---

**Timetable**

*30 minutes before serving:*
  Set the table.
  Put the butter and syrup on the table.

*25 minutes before serving:*
  Start cooking the sausages according to package instructions or
    make the sausages yourself with recipe on page 72.

*20 minutes before serving:*
  Turn on the stove to heat the skillet or griddle.
  Prepare the pancake batter.

*10 minutes before serving:*
  Cook the pancakes.

*5 minutes before serving:*
  Pour the freshly squeezed orange juice into the glasses.
  Place the glasses on the table.

## Shopping List

*Stock Items*

| | |
|---|---|
| butter | baking powder |
| sugar | salt |
| baking soda | Pam (or other nonstick spray) |
| flour | |

*Special Purchases*

freshly squeezed orange juice (This can be purchased already squeezed, or you can buy the oranges and squeeze them your-self. Be sure to allow extra time if you are going to squeeze them yourself.)

sausages—turkey (ones with less fat)

2 apples

1 quart buttermilk

### ∽ Homemade Apple Pancakes

Serves 4

| | |
|---|---|
| 2 eggs | 1½ teaspoons baking powder |
| 1½ cups buttermilk | ½ teaspoon baking soda |
| 3 tablespoons butter, melted | ½ teaspoon salt |
| 1½ cups flour | 1 tablespoon lemon juice |
| 1 tablespoon sugar | 2 apples, peeled and grated |

Heat skillet or griddle over medium heat.

Use a medium-size bowl and an electric beater (if you have one; if not, use the old-fashioned way of a fork or a wire whisk), and beat the eggs until they are well blended. Add the buttermilk, melted butter, flour, sugar, baking powder, baking soda, salt, and lemon juice and beat until the mixture is smooth. Add the grated apple and stir with a spoon until the batter is well blended.

Test the skillet or griddle to check that it is hot enough. Keep your hand high enough above the hot surface to avoid burning yourself (about five inches) and flick a few drops of water off your fingertips onto the hot surface. If the drops bounce and "dance" on the hot surface, it is hot enough to cook the pancakes. Spray the griddle surface with a light coat of Pam (or any other brand of nonstick spray).

Using a large spoon or a ¼-cup measure, pour the batter onto the hot surface. As each pancake spreads, it should be about 4 inches in diameter. Be careful to keep the pancakes from touching one another. When the pancakes are puffy and full of bubbles, they are ready to be turned over. Once they are turned, cook them for a few more minutes or until they are nicely browned. Serve the pancakes with sausages on individual plates with butter and syrup passed separately.

## Kids' Helps

Let the children set the table using the nicest tableware. If they know how to crack eggs, let them crack the eggs and empty them into the bowl. They can beat the eggs and then beat the batter after the remaining ingredients have been added. With your guidance, the other children can turn the sausages to keep them from browning too heavily on one side, and they can pour the pancake batter onto the cooking surface. When the pancakes are ready to be turned over, the children can flip them over.[3]

### ❧ *Whipped Butter*

Whipped butter has 20 fewer calories per tablespoon than butter, and is easier to spread. It is simple to make your own with soft butter. The added air whipped into the butter will increase the volume by about one-third. Serve in an attractive bowl or on a small round plate.

*Amount:* about ⅔ cup

1. Bring to room temperature until very soft, or soften in micro-wave on simmer for about 35 seconds:

    1 cube (½ cup) butter

2. Place butter in small deep mixing bowl and whip vigorously with a wire whisk until light and creamy.

## ∞ Maple Syrup

Real or pure maple syrup comes from real maple trees! It is admittedly expensive, but a little goes a long way, especially when served with fruit topping alternatives. Allow a serving of 2 tablespoons to ¼ cup per person. A pint will serve 12 to 16 people.[4]

---

**Mother's Day Dinner**

*Lemon Garlic Roast Chicken
with Potatoes*

*Table Queen Squash
with Green Peas*

*Blueberry Buckle*

Serves 4

---

## Timetable

*2 hours before serving:*
    Prepare the chicken so it's ready for the oven.
    Peel the potatoes.
    Prepare the squash so it's ready for the oven.

*1½ hours before serving:*
    Preheat the oven to 350°.

*1¼ hours before serving:*
> Place the chicken in preheated oven.
> Prepare the Blueberry Buckle.

*1 hour before serving:*
> Place the squash and the Blueberry Buckle in the oven.
> Baste the chicken and potatoes.

*30 minutes before serving:*
> Set the table.
> Baste the chicken and potatoes again.

*10 minutes before serving:*
> Cook the peas according to package directions.
> Baste the chicken and potatoes a third time.
> Remove the Blueberry Buckle from the oven and set aside.

*To serve:*
> Using poultry shears, cut the chicken into fourths. Usually children enjoy the leg portions, while Mom and Dad prefer the larger breast portions. Place the chicken pieces and potatoes on each plate and top with some pan drippings. Turn the squash right-side up so they are like little bowls. Place a squash on each plate and fill the squash bowl with peas. Add a slice of butter to each.

## Shopping List

*Stock Items*

| | |
|---|---|
| whole garlic | salt |
| pepper | olive oil |
| butter | shortening |
| sugar | egg |
| flour | baking powder |
| milk | cinnamon |

*Special Purchases*
> 3-pound whole chicken
> 2 table queen or acorn squash
> 1 10-ounce package frozen peas
> 1 basket fresh blueberries (1 pint)
> 1 lemon

## ∞ *Lemon Garlic Roast Chicken with Potatoes*

*Preheat oven to 350°.*

> 3-pound whole chicken
> 1 lemon
> 8 cloves garlic (cloves are the small sections of
>     the whole garlic)
> salt
> pepper
> 2 tablespoons olive oil
> 2 tablespoons butter
> 8 small red potatoes, peeled

Remove the inside pieces from the chicken and rinse it under cold water. Pat the chicken dry with paper towels. Cut the lemon into 8 wedge-shaped pieces. Rub the cut lemons over the outside of the chicken. Combine the lemon pieces with the garlic cloves and place inside the chicken. Generously sprinkle the outside of the chicken with salt and pepper. Place the chicken in a roasting pan and place the potatoes around it. In a small bowl, melt the butter in the microwave (about one minute) and add the olive oil to the butter. Pour the combined butter and olive oil over the chicken and potatoes. Place the chicken in the preheated oven and cook for one hour and 15 minutes, basting frequently with the pan juices. Basting is easiest if you use a bulb baster. Simply insert the tip of the baster into the juices, squeeze the bulb, and release it to draw the juices into the baster. Hold the tip over the chicken and squeeze the bulb again to release the juices over the chicken. The roasting pan may need to be tipped to allow the juices to collect in one corner before using the bulb baster.

## ∾ Table Queen Squash with Green Peas

    2 table queen or acorn squash
    1 10-ounce package of frozen peas
    butter

Cut the squash in half. Using a spoon, scrape the inside of the squash to remove the seeds. Using a pan large enough to hold the four halves, place the squash open-side down in the pan. Add enough water to cover the bottom of the pan with about ¼ inch of water. Place the squash in the oven and cook for 1 hour. Ten minutes before serving, prepare the peas according to the package instructions. When both the squash and peas are cooked, place each squash, cut-side up, on a plate, fill the bowl of the squash with peas, and top the peas with a slice of butter.

## ∾ Blueberry Buckle

*Preheat oven to 350°.*

    ½ cup shortening, such as Crisco
    ½ cup sugar
    1 egg
    2 cups flour
    2½ teaspoons baking powder
    ¼ teaspoon salt
    ½ cup milk
    1 basket fresh blueberries (1 pint)

*Topping:*
    ½ cup sugar
    ½ cup flour

½ teaspoon cinnamon
¼ cup butter

In a large bowl, beat the egg with an electric beater. Add the shortening and sugar and beat well until they are blended and have a creamy texture.

In a small bowl, using a pastry blender, combine the remaining sugar, flour, cinnamon, and butter until they have a crumbly consistency and are well blended. Sprinkle the topping over the blueberries and bake in a preheated 350° oven for 45 to 50 minutes. Let cool slightly before serving. To serve the Blueberry Buckle, cut it into squares and serve on plates. It may be topped with ice cream, if desired.

## Kids' Helps

Children can rub the outside of the chicken with the lemons and stuff the inside of the chicken with the combined lemon and garlic. They can sprinkle the chicken with salt and pepper and pour the butter and olive oil over the chicken and potatoes. Older children can peel the potatoes.

Squash are a little bit difficult to work with, but older children can scrape the seeds from the inside of the squash. Once the squash and peas are cooked, children can spoon the peas into the squash bowls.

If they know how, let the children crack the egg for the Blueberry Buckle and empty it into the bowl. They can beat the egg and continue doing all the beating for this recipe. And they can sift the dry ingredients. Let them sprinkle the blueberries over the batter and then sprinkle the topping over the blueberries.[5]

# ⤚Prayer Requests⤙

| Date | Request | Scripture | Update/Answer | Date |
|------|---------|-----------|---------------|------|
|      |         |           |               |      |
|      |         |           |               |      |
|      |         |           |               |      |
|      |         |           |               |      |
|      |         |           |               |      |
|      |         |           |               |      |
|      |         |           |               |      |
|      |         |           |               |      |
|      |         |           |               |      |
|      |         |           |               |      |
|      |         |           |               |      |
|      |         |           |               |      |
|      |         |           |               |      |
|      |         |           |               |      |
|      |         |           |               |      |
|      |         |           |               |      |
|      |         |           |               |      |
|      |         |           |               |      |
|      |         |           |               |      |
|      |         |           |               |      |
|      |         |           |               |      |
|      |         |           |               |      |
|      |         |           |               |      |
|      |         |           |               |      |

# ∽ Sermon Notes ∽

Date:          Speaker:

Title:

Text:

# ❧Notes❧

**Subject:**

# 6

## Father's Day

"GRANDCHILDREN ARE THE CROWN of old men, and the glory of sons is their fathers" (Proverbs 17:6).

**When Observed:** Third Sunday in June
**Earliest Observance:** July 5, 1908; Fairmont, West Virginia

Father's Day is a relatively new holiday in America. It is a day set aside to honor our living fathers; however, many people do use this day to remember those fathers who have died. Instilling both Mother's Day and Father's Day traditions in youngsters is often the role of the "other" parent. Even though the honoree is not the parent of the parent, children first need to see an example of loving-kindness of parents toward each other in order to imitate it.

A number of persons have unconnectedly figured in the growth of Father's Day. The earliest mention we have of a day for fathers is July 5, 1908, when a Father's Day service was held in the Central Church of Fairmont, West Virginia, by Dr. Robert T. Webb at the request of Charles Clayton.

In 1912 at the suggestion of the Reverend J.H. Berringer, pastor of the Irvington Methodist Church, the people of Vancouver, Washington, conducted a Father's Day celebration. They believed it to be the first such ceremony.

Another important figure in the "honor fathers" movement was Harry C. Meet, past president of the Uptown Lions Club of

Chicago, who said that he first had the idea for Father's Day in 1915. He began to suggest it in speeches before various Lions Clubs, and the notion took hold. Members set the date for Father's Day on the third Sunday in June—the Sunday nearest Meek's birthday. The Lions crowned him "Originator of Father's Day."

Father's Day most influential promoter was Mrs. John Bruce Dodd of Spokane, Washington. Her father, William Jackson Smart, had accomplished the amazing task of raising six children alone after his wife died at an early age. Mrs. Dodd wanted to honor him for this unselfish feat.

President Calvin Coolidge recommended the national observance of this day in 1924, though President Woodrow Wilson had officially approved the idea as early as 1916.

The rose is the official Father's Day flower—a white rose for remembrance, and a red rose as a tribute to a living father.

In 1972 the day finally was established permanently when President Richard Nixon signed a Congressional resolution. His action eliminated the need for an annual designation and put Father's Day on the same continuing basis as Mother's Day. Giving gifts has become a natural part of the occasion, and greetings for fathers, grandfathers, uncles, brothers, sons, other relatives, and friends are widely sent. Father's Day has become another happy occasion for family dinners and gatherings. This day is an occasion to establish more intimate relations between fathers and their children, and to impress upon fathers the full measure of their responsibilities and obligations.

*I am a family man and I think that family relationships are the purest, cleanest, whitest sand of all*—Bob Benson.

# What a Father!

Last year I had some extra time at the Dallas-Fort Worth airport waiting for a connecting flight to California, so I decided to purchase a Sunday morning newspaper. While looking through the classified section, I came upon a tribute to a father from a bereaved daughter. As I read this, I commented to myself, "What a father!"

This is an open letter to my father which I desire to share with those of you who did not have the privilege of knowing him. J.T. Yates was a war hero of the European Campaign fighting in the Battle of the Bulge. He landed in France on D Day and fought his way across Europe not only as a medic but also as a combat soldier putting his life in jeopardy constantly while trying to save others. He was a man of his own will and lived his life according to his own beliefs and convictions.

But he was also a hero to me as only a daughter can know and love a father. He was my teacher, whether it be from learning how to survive in the wilderness, to catching a fish, planting a garden, writing a school drama, making science projects, or caring for animals. Unknowingly he strengthened my admiration and appreciation of him. He was my place of safety whenever he held me and cradled me in his big, strong arms. Daddy always tried to give me joy. We made every circus that came to town, walked in every parade, rode in every rodeo, played ball in the park, or took many walks through the zoo. Even at home, he would play games with me, tell me stories, or camp out in the yard. Every year at Christmas, Santa would come to our house and sit me on his knee, yet not one time did I ever suspect that was my dad. They tried to tell me one time that Santa Claus was make-believe but I knew better. I was fortunate to live with him every day for many years. Daddy always let me shine and have all the glory while he stood behind in the shadows. That was his way.

The world may not have considered him a religious man, but he did believe in God. If he couldn't go to church with me, he always provided me a way. Daddy respected men of the clergy and on Sunday afternoons there was always plenty of food for any of God's people that would visit. His love for children was unsurpassed by no one, and there were lots of wiener roasts and entertainment for all youth. That foundation stayed with me and carried me through the next forty years of my life.

Daddy was a man of strong convictions. He never turned his head and pretended not to see. He would stand up to any man, stand up for any woman, stand with any child, and stand behind his beliefs. Daddy was always there when I needed him, and his love was always enough.

If he could, he would have spared me pain, cried my tears to protect all sadness from my eyes. If he could, he would have walked with me everywhere I went to make sure I never chose a wrong turn that might bring me harm or defeat. If he could, he would have shielded my innocence from time, but the time he gave me really wasn't his. He could only watch me grow so he could love me for who I was. But Daddy was a wise man. He knew love couldn't be captured or protected. So he let me take my chances, he gave me my freedom, he let me fight my own battles. I made mistakes but he was always patient.

He was the most generous and giving man of his own self I have ever known, and I hope the legacy he left me will be passed to multitudes of generations.

Thank you, Daddy, for all the times and the nurturing you have given me. The memories will always be in my mind. Now that there will be no more rainbows for us, I will have to let you go, Daddy, but I will always love you. Your daughter, Paula Yates Sugg.[1]

This dad certainly reflected great qualities of character—ones that we all could model for our own lives. Our heavenly Father far exceeds the goodness of our earthly fathers. Unfortunately, many of us may not have had a pleasant experience with our earthly fathers. In some cases, this has prevented us from being able to trust an unseen heavenly Father.

We certainly have the opportunity to experience the abundance of God if we are willing to ask Him. Your Father in heaven is waiting to give you good gifts if you will ask Him.

Today would be a great time to begin trusting your heavenly Father for all your needs. Go to Him in prayer with thanksgiving, adoration, confession, and petition. He is able to meet you where you are.

## Spiritual Teachings

Fathers play such a large part in developing the awareness of God's authority. Children learn this by watching their father's everyday words and actions. I have always tried to model in front of (and behind) our children the respect that we give fatherhood. Some of those traits are: love, respect, submission, godliness, speaking at all times with admiration, honoring his position of leadership, and respecting his decision-making responsibilities.

---

*If I am an effective father, it is because I have deliberately set as one of my priorities the creation of conditions in my home that will stimulate my children to grow to their full potential*—Gordon MacDonald.

---

Exodus 20:12 states, "Honor your father and your mother." I've attempted to teach our children at home to give proper honor to their father. We have honored him through obeying him in his position of authority; being careful of language used in the home; and by showing kindness, politeness, discipline, etc. As our children have grown older, they are more in love with their father than ever before. Not because he is always right or sinless, but because children receive blessings by honoring their father. This is not easy at all times, because obedience often isn't easy. We make a deliberate choice to honor our fathers. As mothers, we can be of great assistance to our children and family developing the harmony that is necessary to build a warm and loving family.

I have learned over the years to make every day of the year Father's Day. Fathers play such a large part in making a family successful in the sight of God. Except for God Himself, our next priority is the father of our home. We need to make a deliberate effort each day to find time for the men of our homes. If we don't have a husband or father at home because of some circumstance, we might want to adopt another man to help out in these times. If the children's real father is alive, we need to encourage them to take time on this day to say, "I love you."

## A Letter from Our Son

We cherish a letter we received from our son, Brad, while he was in college. It reads:

Dear Mom and Dad,

As I sit here studying for my finals, I need to take a break and write you a note to express how much I appreciate the time you have given me over the years. I would not be here studying in college if it wasn't for you giving your time to encourage me along the way. As I think about the money you invested in my college education, I am aware of the many hours that Dad had to work to provide this time in my life.

I remember back to elementary school when you both always attended my school's open house, many times after you had already spent a long day at work. You both took me down to the City Council one evening when I received the award for being the best athlete at East Bluff Park. I also remember you taking me down to the fire station to teach me a lesson after

I set fire to my mattress while foolishly playing with matches. I know you weren't happy about that, but you were there.

Remember all the swim meets, and the little league games that lasted until 10:00 P.M.? It got cold and foggy some evenings, but you were both there cheering me on until the last out.

In junior high you were there with your time and car to take my first girlfriends to school functions. There were more ball games, tournaments, long trips, cold bleachers, sweaty gyms—but you were there.

You really gave a lot of time in high school—attending ball games, transporting me to school and church activities, and sponsoring my youth groups. You were even at the car wash when only a few students showed up, washing and drying cars until you were so tired at day's end. Both of you attended booster club meetings after the football games to catch a glimpse of me on the films making a good catch or tackle.

College wasn't much easier on your schedule. You took time to write me, phone me, and visit me. Parents' weekends at the fraternity house were great with you there. My friends really liked that you were with me. They think you're great! Many of their parents didn't find the time to visit on those weekends. I guess they were too busy, but you weren't. Thanks for all that. You were there.

Yes, Mom and Dad, you always gave me time, but the best thing I remember you giving me was your prayers and godly advice. Many times I could have gone astray, but with each opportunity I looked around and you were there. I will always appreciate the time you gave me. I only hope that one day I will be able to return the favor by giving my wife and children the time you so graciously gave me.

Well, it's time to get back to my marketing notes. I love you both very much.

Love,
Brad

# Father's Day Ideas

1. *Designer Dad*—A crayon drawing of Dad translates into an exclusive, designer T-shirt. The artist should use dark colors and a heavy hand with the crayons on a separate piece of paper. DAD must be written in mirror image to appear correctly on the shirt. Place the crayon drawing on a white T-shirt and iron at cotton temperature.

2. *Cards*—Help the children design and make their own Father's Day cards. Dads love homemade cards with handwritten messages. They all say, "I love you."

---

*Never help a child with a task at which
he feels he can succeed*—M. Montessori.

---

3. *Just Daddy and Me*—At church you might want to plan a brunch just for the fathers and their daughters. Have each share introductions, good food (physical as well as spiritual), and a fun time with each other. It is their special date on this special day.

4. *Kidnap Dad*—Create a plan for kidnapping your dad from work to have lunch together. (You might need some help from Mom to pull this off.)

5. *Popcorn Pop*—Fix and eat together a bowl of popcorn. (Try it without TV—try conversation instead.)

6. *Gifts of Self*—None of the following gift suggestions costs anything, yet each is one-of-a-kind and bound to please because it's a gift of yourself. Every day should be a day in which we honor all members of our family, but this day should be special just for Father.

✦ *The gift of a compliment*—Perhaps you could make a list of the qualities you admire in your father: his sense of humor; his survival instinct; his ability to live without impossible expectations; his provision for the family; his godly attributes; his warmth, affection, kindness, and unselfishness.

✦ *A gift of affection*—How about a warm embrace, a kiss on the cheek, a moment to hold his hand? All of us need affection, no matter what our age or how much we protest that it's not our style.

✦ *A gift of forgiveness*—People are not perfect. Those closest to us often seem the least so. We owe them the same forgiveness we expect for our own imperfections. An act of forgiveness can start things anew and reunite us as nothing else can.

✦ *A gift of thanks*—Tell Dad how much you appreciate all that he does for the family. We know that there are days he doesn't feel like going to work but he does. He plays catch and chases our errant throws but never complains. He provides great trips at winter and summer time for our vacations. Gee, Dad, thanks, thanks, thanks!

✦ *A gift of listening*—Take Dad aside and have him share about his childhood and what were some of his memories, fears, goals, and aspirations. Let Dad just talk about himself, and you be the interested listener. This would be a great time to ask him those questions you always wanted to ask but didn't have the time.

✦ *A gift of laughter*—Have Dad tell you his best jokes; be prepared to have a few of your own ready. Here are a couple to get started:

> Dad: Did you hear about the old lady who told knitting jokes?

Son: No, I haven't.

Dad: She was a real nitwit.

◆ ◆ ◆

Dad: Did you hear about the thief who stole a calendar?

Daughter: What happened to him?

Dad: He got 12 months.

◆ ◆ ◆

Dad: Did you hear about the horse who ate an electric wire instead of hay?

Son: That's shocking!

Dad: He went haywire.[2]

7. *Special treats*—If you live at home with Dad, talk with Mom and plan some special activities for him. Really make a big deal out of this day.

  ◆ Treat Dad to breakfast in bed.

  ◆ A delightful gift if you are low on money is to give Dad a cute coupon stating that it is good for one free washing of the family car, one free back rub, one shoe shine, or free time to read the newspaper with no interruptions.

  ◆ Plan a picnic for Dad.

  ◆ Take Dad out to brunch after church (be sure to make reservations first).

  ◆ Tell Dad he doesn't have to do any work on this special day.

8. *Long-distance appreciation*—If you no longer live at home, you still need to take time to honor Dad.

+ Send him a hanging plant for the patio or a plant for his office.

+ Give him a telephone call. (Since the telephone lines are extremely busy on Father's Day, you might try to make the call the day before.)

+ Send two tickets for a sporting event, musical concert, or some other activity he would enjoy.

9. *Read Proverbs to me*—If you are a teenage boy, ask your father to read the book of Proverbs to you. There are 31 chapters, and you can read one each day. My Bob did this for our son when he was 15, and it provides a great time together for father and son (daughters can also be included).

---

*Tis a happy thing to be a father unto many sons*
—William Shakespeare.

---

10. *Gifts of special tools*—Many times Dad is in special need of some tools for his garage or automobile. Remember those times when he has said, "I sure wish I had _____, it would make my job so much easier." Those are cue words for a future gift list. Dads are practical in nature and really appreciate practical gifts. Take this opportunity to make Father feel very special on this, his day. The following acrostic is what FATHER means to me:

## F ∽ Faithful Follower of Christ

An honorable father is a faithful follower of Christ. In Matthew 11:30 (NIV) we read, "For my yoke is easy and my burden is light." If fathers follow Jesus, they will escape from the hard yoke of living by their own laws as they submit to the kindly yoke of

Christ Jesus. Only the man who follows the command of Jesus and lets His yoke rest upon him finds the Lord's burden easy, and under its gentle pressure receives the power to persevere in the right way. The commands of Jesus are hard for the disobedient, but for those who willingly submit, the yoke is easy and the burden is light. Jesus asks nothing of us without first giving us the strength to perform it. His commandments never destroy life; they strengthen and heal it. Our country desperately needs fathers to stand up and be counted. Our sons and daughters need to know who their heavenly and earthly fathers are.

## A ∞ Allows God to Make Him All He Can Be

One of the hardest lessons about trusting God in our lives is to allow God to be the change agent in dads. Far too often the family wants to be the change agent. Dads need to have space to come to God on His terms and in His timing. It's amazing what happens to Dad when we let God deal with him on His schedule and not ours. In order to do this, we have to concentrate on the positives and let God deal with the negatives.

> *When I was a boy of fourteen my father was so ignorant I could hardly stand to have him around. But when I got to be twenty-one, I was astonished at how much the old man had learned*—Mark Twain.

Become an encourager and cheerleader for Dad. Be excited about his successes. Comfort him when the contract isn't signed, when the deal falls through, and when sickness slows him down. A dad needs permission to fail on occasion. Where else but in the home can he do that? Continue to pray for Dad each day. Encourage the children to be a part of that prayer for Dad's specific needs.

## T ⌐ *Thanks God for All His Blessings*

In Deuteronomy 8:18 (NIV) we read, "But remember the LORD your God, for it is he who gives you the ability to produce wealth," and Proverbs 28:20 (NIV) states, "A faithful man will be richly blessed."

---

*I never understood the obstacles my father faced until I became one. I love my father's memory now more than ever*—Author unknown.

---

The beginning of greatness is for a man to realize where everything comes from: God. A godly man will count his blessings, be content where he is, and thank God for all the blessings bestowed upon him. On this special day, we pray that our fathers will have thankful hearts.

## H ⌐ *Holiness in His Approach to Life*

Peter writes in 1 Peter 1:15, "But just as he who called you is holy, so be holy in all you do." What an awesome command! It isn't a common goal for men of the nineties. If fathers today prayed to be holy, strove to be holy, and were holy, we would have a revival like the world has never seen. We would see marriages healed, differences settled, welfare costs curtailed, and unity displayed in America. The cry is for men to be holy. Their love of God and of man cannot be just symbolic—it has to be completely real. It is not just a mental process, but the giving and commitment of themselves as men to God. As a family, be an encourager to fathers to step out in faith that their God can make them holy. Men can be holy in the nineties. Maybe not easily, but what is easy that has any real value?

## E ∞ Expresses Love to Those Around Him

When Jesus was asked by a young lawyer in Matthew 22:37,39 (NIV) to name the great commandment, Jesus responded, "Love the Lord your God with all your heart and with all your soul and with all your mind. . . . Love your neighbor as yourself." He stated that we should love God, love others, and love ourselves. If fathers could grasp this triangle of love, we would begin to see men of low self-esteem rise above destructive behavior and move into positions of leadership in their homes. This kind of love is a gift we give to others. We can't buy it. It is a decision we make on a daily basis that someone is valuable and special to us. What better day than this special day to tell Dad that he is special?

In our household we honor special people with a red memory plate that reads, "You Are Special Today." We serve their meal (breakfast, lunch, or dinner) on it, and during the meal each person around the table shares why our honored guest is so special to him or her. After we complete that cycle, we turn to our special guest and say, "Now tell us why you think you are special." At first this request is very threatening, but after a few moments the person usually comes up with a few statements that reveal why he thinks he is special.

Ask yourself why you are special and see how you would answer that question. Our ten-year-old grandson, Chad, gave us a special answer when he was asked to tell us why he is special. Chad replied, "I am special because I am a child of God." He had it absolutely right. We are special because of that eternal relationship with God—we are His children!

## R ∞ Responds to God's Teachings in Scripture

A father is a man who not only hears God's Word, but who also lets it penetrate into his heart and soul. We want men who will give testimony to what God means in their everyday lives: in marriage, as a father, with a neighbor, at the job, and at church.

We desire fathers who are not afraid to be called by Jesus to stand up for His teachings in Scripture—not Sunday Christians, but men who want to live a consistent 24-hours-a-day and seven-days-a-week lifestyle.

A godly father can be trusted because he has endured the tests of the world and has been found true to Christ's calling—a simple man who believes what is revealed in the Holy Scriptures.

The Son of God says this: "I know your deeds, and your love and faith and service and perseverance" (Revelation 2:18,19).

If we had fathers like this, we could say that they reflect all that God intended when He created man in the garden. Our world needs this kind of man. If fathers reflect these attributes, their families, communities, and churches will raise them up as leaders and will call them blessed.

Recently in our local newspaper there appeared a reprint from a previous Ann Landers article dealing with Father's Day; it originally appeared in the *Danbury* (Connecticut) *News-Times*. I thought it had great wisdom for all of us on this day of celebration:

---

### Father

4 Years:     My daddy can do anything.

7 Years:     My dad knows a lot, a whole lot.

8 Years:     My father doesn't know quite everything.

12 Years:    Oh, well, naturally Father doesn't know that either.

14 Years:    Father? Hopelessly old-fashioned.

21 Years:    Oh, that man is out of date. What did you expect?

25 Years:    He knows a little bit about it, but not much.

30 Years:    Maybe we ought to find out what Dad thinks.

35 Years:    A little patience. Let's get Dad's assessment before we do anything.

| 50 Years: | I wonder what Dad would have thought about that. He was pretty smart. |
|---|---|
| 60 Years: | My Dad knew absolutely everything. |
| 65 Years: | I'd give anything if Dad were here so I could talk this over with him. I really miss that man. |

# A Special Breakfast for Dad

---

**Father's Day Breakfast**

*Turkey Sausage*

*Orange Juice*

*Crunchy Potato Casserole*

*Scrambled Eggs with
Easy Salsa* (optional)

*Toast or Breakfast Biscuits*

Serves 6

---

For Turkey Sausage see recipe on page 72.
For Orange Juice see recipe on page 71.

## ↩ *Crunchy Potato Casserole*

2 pounds frozen hash browns
1 stick melted margarine or butter
1 can cream of chicken soup
8 ounces sour cream
10 ounces grated sharp cheese
½ cup chopped onions
dash of salt and pepper
2 cups corn flakes

Mix the above ingredients together and put in a 9" x 12" casserole. Top with 2 cups corn flakes (crushed) and one stick melted butter or margarine. Bake uncovered at 375° for 45 minutes. This freezes well.

## ∞ Scrambled Eggs

*Amount:* 2 eggs per serving

1. Add to shallow saucepan or frying pan over moderately low heat:
   1½ teaspoons olive oil or butter

2. Whisk together thoroughly with a fork in a bowl (per serving):
   2 eggs
   1 tablespoon water or milk per egg
   ⅛ teaspoon salt (optional)

> *The liquid whisked into the egg will "stretch"
> the protein and make it more tender.*

3. Evenly distribute warmed oil or melted butter over surface of the pan and pour in the eggs.

4. When the eggs begin to set, push the cooked eggs to one side with edge of spatula to let uncooked eggs run underneath. You can also gently turn the eggs over, if you like, but don't stir the eggs. Stirring scrambled eggs breaks them up into unpleasantly textured small lumps and pieces.

5. Remove eggs from heat when just barely set on the top—even a bit undercooked. Do not let the eggs brown on the bottom.

6. Cover with a lid until ready to serve.

*Quantity cooking tip:* For 2 to 3 eggs I use an 8" pan. If eggs are too shallow in the pan, they cook too fast; if too thick (over 1¼" deep), they cook too slowly and require too much stirring. To scramble a large quantity, spray a baking pan with a nonstick spray, cover bottom of pan with melted butter or oil, add eggs, and bake in 350° oven. When they begin to cook around the outside edge, gently loosen the eggs and carefully move them. Continue moving the cooked eggs occasionally, until all are scrambled.

## ∞ *Easy Salsa* (optional)

This takes the work out of salsa-making, yet provides the home-prepared touch, plus more substance in texture and bulk.

*Amount:* about 1¼ cups

Blend amounts as desired, to taste:
    2 small (Roma size) fresh tomatoes, finely chopped
    ¼ small onion, finely chopped
    2 tablespoons bottled salsa, to taste

## ∞ *Breakfast Biscuits*[3]

*Amount:* 10 biscuits
*Preheat oven to 425°.*

1. In medium bowl, blend dry ingredients:
    2 cups whole-wheat pastry flour or white flour
    2½ teaspoons baking powder
    ½ teaspoon baking soda
    ½ teaspoon salt

2. Whisk together in a 2-cup measure or small bowl:
    1 cup buttermilk
    3 tablespoons oil (extra virgin olive oil preferred)

3. Stir liquid ingredients into dry ingredients just until mixed; beat 10 strokes.

4. Drop spoonfuls of dough on ungreased cookie sheet.

5. Bake at 425° for 12 to 15 minutes until lightly golden on the bottom.

---

*A father is the head of a unit of people launched on an exploration of life and all the things God has placed in the world for us to enjoy—*Gordon MacDonald.

7

*Independence Day*

"AND YOU SHALL KNOW the truth, and the truth shall make you free" (John 8:32).

**When Celebrated:** Fourth of July
**First Celebration:** 1776

This is our grand national holiday—the glorious Fourth, when Americans manifest their patriotic enthusiasm in various ways.

The military marks the day by firing a salute of 13 guns and reading the Declaration of Independence. All over the country, church bells are rung in memory of the Liberty Bell that proclaimed independence. This most-famous bell was actually made in England, and around its rim are these prophetic words: "Proclaim liberty throughout the land unto all the inhabitants thereof."

The earliest celebration in 1776 was a very exciting and cheerful occasion. At last the colonies were independent from England. There was yelling and screaming, bonfires were lit, and people paraded and danced in the streets.

---

*Ask not what your country can do you for you; ask what you can do for your country*—John F. Kennedy.

The Fourth of July is still celebrated in much the same fashion: there are parades, dancing, and fireworks (some communities are placing certain restrictions due to possible fire dangers).

Since the Fourth of July falls in the summertime and the children are out of school, parents can take their families on outings in the park, in the country, or to the seashore.

This holiday commemorates the formal adoption of the Declaration of Independence by the Continental Congress in Philadelphia on July 4, 1776. Although the resolution for independence was passed by Congress on July 2 and most of the members did not sign the declaration until August 2, the Fourth of July has always been celebrated as the anniversary of national independence. The president of the Congress, John Hancock, did make it official with his signature on that date.

---

*A good newspaper and Bible in every house, a good schoolhouse in every district, and a church in every neighborhood, all appreciated as they deserve, are the chief support of virtue, morality, civil liberty, and religion*—Ben Franklin.

---

As you and your family celebrate this day, you can elect to be an originator of traditions in your family, or you may elect to join in other people's traditions. Either way, it is a wonderful time of the year. Several ideas follow that might help you do something different this year.

## Activities

1. *Backyard barbecue*—The theme for decorations is so easy: red, white, and blue. All the way from the invitations to the napkins you can carry through the patriotic colors of our flag. Be sure to send your invitations at least four weeks ahead of the event. People make plans early and need time to decide what they are

going to do. Ask your family for suggestions on what the menu will be, what games will be played, and who should be on the guest list. The backyard barbecue can branch out to a park setting if the crowd gets too big. Big is fun for this kind of celebration.

---

*Patriotism is your conviction that this country is superior to all other countries because you were born in it*—George Bernard Shaw.

---

2. *Games*—All kinds of games can be explored for this day. Ask the grandparents what kinds of games they or their parents used to play when they were young. These older and often-forgotten games are a delight. One such old game is called "pick-up sticks" or "Jack straws." Cut any number of sticks of wood ½" x ½" x 14" and paint them three different colors—red, white, and blue. Throw them in a basket or drop them on the ground in a pile. Ask the children to remove one stick at a time without moving the other sticks. You can make up rules depending on the ages of the children and have colorful prizes for the winners.

   A very simple contest that requires only a baseball for equipment is to draw a circle three feet in diameter on the ground and see if anyone can stand at the edge, throw the ball straight up into the air, and have it land back in the circle.

3. *Sack races*—Go to your local grain store and purchase grain sacks (the number you will need depends upon the size of your group). Lay out a course that has a start and a finish line. Have each contestant stand in a sack and hop along the course. The length of the course can vary depending on the ages of participants.

4. *Three-legged race*—This is a similar activity to sack races. However, instead of using a grain bag, have two people stand side by side and tie their inside legs together. The contestants line up

behind the starting line and at "Go" they run and hop their way to the finish line.

5. *Pop bottle fill*—You'll need pop bottles of the same size, a large bucket of water, and paper cups. Place the large bucket of water in the center of a circle of adults who are lying on their backs on the grass with their feet pointing away from the bucket of water and their heads about six feet from the water bucket. The adults, while lying down, place pop bottles on their foreheads. The children are given paper cups. The object is to have the children run to the bucket of water, fill their cups with water, hurry to their parent's pop bottle, and try to empty their cups into the bottle. As you can imagine, the adults will get soaked. Of course, the prize goes to the team that fills the pop bottle first.

6. *Egg toss*—This activity carries the anticipation that the next toss will cover someone with egg. You play with a partner. Have the partners line up facing each other (the distance apart depends upon the ages of the players). Young children will stand close to start out, and older children might be six to ten feet apart.

   Give each team one raw egg in the shell. At the starter's command, the person holding the egg will toss the egg in an underhand motion to his partner to catch. If the egg breaks, the team is eliminated from the game. If not, the partners stay in the game. (If the egg hits the ground but does not break, the partners stay in the game.)

   The starter will give directions for those remaining to step back one giant step. Again, the person makes an underhand toss of the egg. Those who have eggs intact will continue playing the game until one set of partners is left in the game with a good egg. You might want to suggest that the contestants remove their rings. Have some hand towels to clean up any messy egg splashes. You can also substitute water balloons for eggs.

7. *Running events*—These are always great fun for the children. They love to try to win. Be sure to divide the children into age groups so the competition will be fair.

8. *Wheelbarrow races*—Be sure not to have the races too long because the children may not have strong arm muscles. This game is played as a team. One partner holds the other's legs in the air by the ankles and follows behind him as he walks with his hands to the finish line. You might even want to have the partners reverse positions and come back to the start line.

    Remember to have plenty of inexpensive prizes available for the winners. Be sure that all children get participant prizes. It's important that everyone leaves feeling that he or she was a winner.

9. *Parade*—Have a family parade. The children love it. Get pots and pans, tambourines, horns, and toy instruments. Small children can carry a flag or tie colored balloons onto strollers, wagons, and tricycles. Everyone could march around the neighborhood and ask others to join in the parade. For country folks, a hayride would be great fun, or decorate horses and have a parade. This is a nice time when small communities can rally together and have fun. A nice ending to the parade would be an ice-cream social or a hot-dog roast.

10. *Plant a tree*—Decide beforehand what kind of tree you want to plant. Where do you want to plant it—at home, at church, in a city park, or at school? If not planted at home, be sure to get permission from the appropriate personnel. Make sure you know how the tree will be taken care of.

    This gives you a great opportunity to talk to your children about ecology. This could become a yearly tradition for your family.

> *After what I owe to God, nothing should be*
> *more dear or more sacred than the love and*
> *respect I owe to my country*—De Thou.

11. *Make a patriotic cake*—Children love to get into the kitchen and bake. Decide the shape and decor for the cake. (Naturally, you will want to use red, white, and blue colors.) Go to your local party store and purchase flags, candles, stars, etc. for decorating the cake. Serve red punch with ice cubes tinted with blue food coloring. As you cut the cake, you might want one of the children to lead the group in saying the Pledge of Allegiance.

12. *Balloon walk*—Inflate a number of red, white, or blue balloons and draw a holiday design on each with a felt-tip pen. Divide the group into two or more equal-size teams. At the signal, each person must carry the balloon between his knees to the goal line and back. If the balloon breaks, he must come back for a new one and start over. The first team to finish is the winner. A large balloon for each team member would be an appropriate prize.

    *Variations:* 1) Play this as an individual competition, using a stopwatch to time each competitor. The one with the shortest time is the winner. 2) Set up an obstacle course for players to walk through on their way to the goal line.

13. *Straw relay*—Cut two or more four-inch-high holiday shapes from construction paper. Divide the group into two or more equal teams. Give each player a drinking straw, and each team one of the paper shapes. One at a time the team members pick up the shape by sucking through the straw, then carry it to the goal line and back. If they drop it, they must start over. The

first team to have all players complete the task successfully is the winner.

14. *Beanbag relay*—Make two or more holiday-shaped felt bean-bags. Divide the group into two or more equal teams and have each team line up in separate lines with the players one behind the other. Give a beanbag to the first person. Have the team pass the beanbag to the last person in the line and back again. Before each round, the leader calls out the way in which the bag is to be passed: over the head, between the legs, down the right or left. If anyone passes the beanbag incorrectly, it goes back to the front of the line and that team starts over. The first team to get its beanbag back to the first person in line is the winner.

15. *Paper bag pops*—Give each person a lunch-size paper bag and set out some crayons or felt-tip pens. Have participants deco-rate their bags appropriately for the holiday. When bags are completed, divide the group into relay teams. The object of the game is for each person at the front of the line to blow up his bag as he runs toward the end of his line. When he reaches the end of the line he is to pop it. If the sack doesn't pop the first time, he must keep trying until he is successful. The next person in each line repeats the action as soon as he hears the previous bag pop. Play continues until player number one is back at the front of the line.

16. *Spear the sweets*—Put holiday-colored jelly beans into two bowls that have been decorated with self-adhesive holiday seals. Divide the group into two equal relay teams and give each team one bowl. The teams line up and each person is given a round wooden toothpick. At the signal, the first per-son in each line spears a jelly bean with the toothpick and feeds it to the person next to him. He then passes the bowl to the second player who feeds one to the next person, and so on. The team to reach the end of the line first is the winner.

---

**Fourth of July Picnic**

*Pasta Salad*

*Coleslaw* and *Bean Salad*

Grilled Corn in Husks

Tomato and Red Onion Slices
with *Vinaigrette Dressing*

Hot Dogs and Hamburgers

*Flag Cake*

*Three-Layer Chocolate Bars*

*Banana-Walnut Ice Cream*

*Fresh Lemonade*

---

## ✆ Pasta Salad

*Amount:* 8 servings
*Preparation time:* 15 minutes

      1 pound thin spaghetti
      1 8-ounce bottle Italian salad dressing
      2¾-ounce jar Salad Supreme salad seasoning
      2 chopped celery stalks
      1 chopped green pepper
      1 thinly sliced onion
      1 pint cherry tomatoes
      1 6-ounce can pitted ripe olives

1. Cook spaghetti according to package directions. Drain and rinse
   in cold water.

2. Combine spaghetti, salad dressing, and salad seasoning.

3. Add celery, green pepper, and onion.

4. Chill 3 to 4 hours (may do 3 to 4 days ahead).

5. Just before serving, add tomatoes and olives.

## ∞ Coleslaw—"Easy to make for a crowd'

*Amount:* 8 to 10 servings
*Preparation time:* 20 minutes

> 1 grated cabbage head
> 6 grated carrots
> 1 finely chopped green pepper
> 1 minced green onion, optional
> ¼ cup chopped parsley
> ½ cup Miracle Whip salad dressing
> 2 tablespoons sugar
> 1 tablespoon dill weed
> 1½ teaspoons celery seed
> 1 tablespoon rice vinegar
> salt to taste

Mix all ingredients. Refrigerate.

## ∞ Bean Salad

*Amount:* 10 servings (2½ quarts)
*Preparation time:* 30 minutes
*Marinating time:* 6 to 8 hours (must do ahead)

*Salad*

> 1 8-ounce can red kidney beans
> 1 8-ounce can garbanzos
> 1 8-ounce can green beans

1 8-ounce can yellow wax beans
1 diced, large green pepper
2 sliced green onions
1 4-ounce can sliced, black ripe olives
2 tablespoons chopped pimento

*Dressing*

¼ cup vegetable oil
¼ cup lemon juice
¼ cup honey
1 tablespoon soy sauce
1 teaspoon Spice Island salad seasoning

1. Place dressing ingredients in glass jar and shake to mix.

2. Drain all beans.

3. Combine dressing with salad ingredients. Toss well.

4. Marinate in refrigerator for 6 to 8 hours or overnight. Toss occasionally.

## ◌ Vinaigrette Dressing

*Amount:* 12 to 15 servings
*Preparation time:* 45 minutes

1 cup olive oil
2 tablespoons lemon juice
4 tablespoons vinegar
2 tablespoons Dijon mustard
1 minced garlic clove
1 tablespoon chopped fresh basil
1 tablespoon chopped fresh tarragon
1 tablespoon chopped fresh oregano
Season to taste

Combine above ingredients. Mix well.

## ∞ *Flag Cake*—"Serve with pride"

*Amount:* 12 to 15 servings
*Preparation time:* 45 minutes

    1 white cake mix
    1 cup heavy cream
    1 tablespoon sugar
    ½ teaspoon vanilla
    ½ cup fresh blueberries
    2 cups sliced, fresh strawberries

1. Mix and bake cake according to package directions in 9" x 13" baking dish.

2. Place cake on attractive serving dish or platter.

3. Beat cream until soft peaks form. Add sugar and vanilla.

4. Spread whipped cream in an even layer over top of cake.

5. Place 2 lines of blueberries at right angles in top left corner to form a 4-inch square. Fill square with additional lines of blueberries. Leave small amount of white cream showing between the berries.

6. Use overlapping sliced strawberries to form horizontal red stripes from side to side on cake, allowing cream to show for white stripes.

7. Refrigerate cake until serving time.

## ∞ *Three-Layer Chocolate Bars*—"So good they're almost sinful"

*Preparation time:* 45 minutes
*Baking time:* 25 to 30 minutes

*Crust*
    ½ cup butter

2 ounces unsweetened chocolate
1 cup sugar
1 cup flour
1 teaspoon baking powder
1 teaspoon vanilla
2 eggs
1 cup chopped nuts

1. Melt the butter and chocolate.

2. Add remaining ingredients. Mix thoroughly.

3. Pour into greased 9" x 13" baking dish.

*Filling*

1 8-ounce package softened cream cheese
½ cup sugar
2 tablespoons flour
¼ cup softened butter
1 egg
1 teaspoon vanilla
½ cup chopped nuts
1 6-ounce package semisweet chocolate chips

1. Combine and beat filling ingredients, except nuts and chocolate chips, until smooth (about 1 minute).

2. Stir nuts into filling. Pour over crust.

3. Sprinkle chocolate chips on top of filling.

4. Bake at 350° for 25 to 30 minutes.

*Frosting*

¼ cup butter
2 ounces unsweetened chocolate
2 ounces softened cream cheese
¼ cup milk

3 cups powdered sugar
1 teaspoon vanilla
2 cups miniature marshmallows

1. Melt butter and chocolate.

2. Add cream cheese and milk.

3. Stir in powdered sugar and vanilla.

4. Stir in marshmallows.

*To Assemble*

1. Frost while hot.

2. Cool and cut into bars.

## ∞ *Banana-Walnut Ice Cream*—"Mmm—Good!"

*Amount:* 1 gallon
*Preparation time:* 10 minutes
*Freezing time:* 30 minutes

4 cups sour cream
4 cans sweetened condensed milk
8 cups half-and-half (may use half milk)
6 mashed or chopped bananas
1 cup chopped walnuts

1. Mix all ingredients.

2. Process in ice-cream freezer.

## ∞ *Fresh Lemonade*[1]

*Amount:* 1 cup
*Preparation time:* 15 minutes

*Cooking time:* 2 minutes

For each cup of water, use:
    3–4 tablespoons sugar
    1½ tablespoons lemon juice

1. Boil water and sugar 2 minutes. Chill.

2. Add lemon juice.

## Invitation

The invitation is written in white ink on a red card outlined with blue-and-gold star stickers. A small American flag may be included.

A firecracker invitation is created by covering an empty tissue roll with red paper. Information is inside and attached to an 8-inch wick of heavy string with a tag that reads "Pull." Hand deliver.

## Decorations or Setting the Mood

Line the entrance of your home with several American flags to greet guests with a patriotic spirit.

Clusters of red, white, and blue balloons with crepe paper streamers can decorate the party area.

## Table Setting and Centerpiece

The buffet table is covered with a red or white tablecloth. Blue paper napkins are encircled with napkin rings made of white construction paper, affixed with a large gold star. Red and white paper plates and cups complete the table setting.

An "Uncle Sam" hat filled with red and white petunias makes a patriotic centerpiece. A small toy drum with one end removed may be used as a serving dish. Place small flags around the rim. The table can also be enhanced by a watermelon cannon.

# 8

# Thanksgiving

*"ALWAYS GIVE THANKS for everything . . . in the name of our Lord Jesus Christ"* (Ephesians 5:20 TLB).

**When Observed:** Fourth Thursday in November
**Earliest Observance:** 1621 in Plymouth, Massachusetts

The Pilgrims, who in 1621 observed our first Thanksgiving holiday in Plymouth, Massachusetts, were thankful for their harvest in the New World. They had suffered a perilous journey on the Mayflower, a dreadfully cold winter, and a large number of deaths. By most standards, the first harvest was very mediocre. Many of the first crops were failures. This first Thanksgiving lasted for three days and was celebrated with enthusiasm. The menu was extensive and the food abundant. The Indian braves had added five deer to the store of meat. The pilgrims had venison, duck, goose, seafood, eels, white bread, corn bread, leeks, watercress, and a variety of greens. Wild plums and dried berries were served for dessert. Although turkeys were plentiful, there is no record that they were eaten on this first Thanksgiving holiday.

---

The first Thanksgiving proclamation was made by Governor Bradford three years after the Pilgrims settled at Plymouth:

*To all ye Pilgrims:*

*Inasmuch as the great Father has given us this year an abundant harvest of Indian corn, wheat, peas, beans, squashes, and garden vegetables, and has made the forests to abound with game and the sea with fish and clams, and inasmuch as he has protected us from the ravages of the savages, has spared us from pestilence and disease, has granted us freedom to worship God according to the dictates of our own conscience; now I, your magistrate, do proclaim that all ye Pilgrims, with your wives and ye little ones, do gather at ye meeting house, on ye hill, between the hours of 9 and 12 in the day time, on Thursday, November ye 29th, of the year of our Lord one thousand six-hundred and twenty-three, and the third year since ye Pilgrims landed on ye Pilgrim Rock, there to listen to ye pastor and render thanksgiving to ye Almighty God for all his blessings.*

—William Bradford, Ye Governor of Ye Colony.

Records of subsequent Thanksgiving celebrations are rather sporadic. Many of the later colonies did not adopt this harvest celebration. The first national Thanksgiving proclamation was issued by George Washington in 1789. Mrs. Sarah Josepha Hale of Boston had a great deal of influence on the government toward having this day celebrated across the nation. In 1863 President Abraham Lincoln made a proclamation to establish Thanksgiving Day as a national holiday to be observed on the last Thursday of November. In 1941 Congress changed this to the fourth Thursday in November.

For the last 100 years in America, we have begun to develop some meaningful traditions to make this one of the most memorable of all our holidays. Thanksgiving is warm hearts, good food, family, and lots of conversation. However, some people don't have these kinds of memories.

I was talking with a woman at one of my seminars who had memories of absolutely nothing. Thanksgiving wasn't different from any other day. Today she creates memories, making them on purpose. "We talk about what we can do for others weeks before

Thanksgiving," she said. "The children become a part of special giving times."

---

*Tis the season for kindling the fire of hospitality in the hall, the genial fire of charity in the heart*—Washington Irving.

One Thanksgiving a family went to skid row in downtown Los Angeles and helped serve Thanksgiving dinner. They'll never forget that day. It was such a joy that the children suggested they do it again for Christmas.

One year Bob and I were doing a holiday seminar at a very alive church in the heart of a low economic area in El Monte, California. It was November 20, and the church was full. The ladies of the church were in a back room busily pulling food from shopping bags. We were so busy ourselves setting up tables and seminar props that we didn't really take notice of exactly what they were doing.

After the first half of my presentation and the refreshments, the ladies did a wonderful thing. Women came from that back room carrying the most beautiful Thanksgiving "love baskets" filled with the complete ingredients for a Thanksgiving dinner from fruit to turkey and pumpkin pies, 32 baskets in all. They then proceeded to hand them out to each single person there.

As I watched those people come forward to receive their baskets, I saw eyes filled with tears: single working parents, single college students, some people who obviously didn't have finances for such a meal. That church wanted to give and create a memory, and they sure did. Among the group was a young man who played the piano that day for the singing time. His wife had left him with three young children, and he was currently unemployed and living in a small rented apartment. When he went forward to receive his basket, he sobbed with joy. Bob and I were touched by the beauty of that day. We had so much and had taken so much for granted.

If you don't know of a needy family, find one. Call the Salvation Army or a local church and ask them how to get in touch with a needy family. Then decide ways you can help make a special memory for that family this holiday.

Since Thanksgiving preparation can take up such a large part of November, you might want to use one of our calendar pages (see sample at end of chapter) and jot down what needs to be done in little bits and pieces to make this a manageable time rather than a stressful one. Starting with the first week in November, delegate each day to accomplish some of these activities.

## First Week in November

As we approach the first week in November, we can begin our holiday organization. Use the "First Week" form at the end of this chapter. Creating memories takes time, and organization for the holidays will give us the time we need.

To polish your silver, add one tablespoon of ammonia to your silver polish. You'll get a super shine, plus it prolongs the shine well into the new year. So do it early and enjoy beautiful silver for the holidays.

Toothpaste on a damp cloth is also good silver polish for the last-minute spoon you forgot that you want to put in the cranberry sauce dish.

Early in the month invite your guests for Thanksgiving dinner. A cheery phone invitation or a written invitation is always welcome.

## Second Week in November

Use the "Second Week" form at the end of this chapter to plan this second week. Make up your Thanksgiving dinner menu at the same time you compile your marketing list. You can pick up the dry goods and staples for your meal now (stuffing mix, cranberry sauce, applesauce, water chestnuts, etc.). It's easier on the budget and makes shopping faster later. Check off items on your marketing list as you purchase them. Don't forget the parsley for garnishes. Parsley stays fresh for weeks if rinsed well and wrapped in a paper towel. Put it into a plastic storage bag, pressing the air out and sealing the sack tightly.

Plan your Thanksgiving table setting and centerpiece early. Check your silver pieces, plates, and serving dishes to be sure you have enough for the number of guests you are inviting.

Table decoration can be easy and creative. Take large apples and core out enough to hold a votive candle. Squeeze lemon juice around the cutout area and then insert the candle. The apples can be set in front of each person's place or down the center of the table with autumn leaves, pods, grapes, pears, corn, eggplant, and even squash and nuts. When the candles are lit, you'll have a beautiful harvest display. Plus, after Thanksgiving you can use the parts of the centerpiece for a fruit salad or soup.

If you don't have votive candles, use tall tapers or whatever you have available. (This idea can be used for Christmas with red and green apples.)

Here's an activity with a purpose: Take the children or grandchildren on a harvest walk and collect fall leaves of all sizes. Talk about the different colors and shapes of the leaves. Also collect pods that have fallen from the trees. Carefully put them in a bag or basket and bring them home. The leaves can be dipped in melted paraffin, laid on wax paper, and then used for your harvest table decorations. The pods and small leaves—along with nuts, plastic grapes, small silk flowers, and even an artificial bird—can be used in making a hat for your pumpkin. Find a whole pumpkin that is sort of fat and squatty, but do not cut into it. With a hot-glue gun, glue to the top of the pumpkin a nesting-type material, like gray moss or sphagnum moss. On top of that, glue small leaves, nuts, flowers, a bow, or silk flowers. This can be used as a centerpiece with the apples, figurines of pilgrims, etc.

You and the family will be so proud of this masterpiece, and it will last for several weeks. When Thanksgiving is over, simply pry off the hat and store it until next year to put on top of a new pumpkin.

*Speak to one another with psalms, hymns and spiritual songs. Sing and make music in your heart to the Lord, always giving thanks to God the Father for everything, in the name of our Lord Jesus Christ*—Ephesians 5:19,20 (NIV).

Name cards can also be completed ahead of time. Every year we, as a family, find verses with a thankfulness theme. Take a 3" x 5" card and fold it in half and stand it on the table. On the front write the name of the person who will sit at that place and inside write a Thanksgiving Scripture. When everyone is seated, each person then reads his verse—that can be the table blessing.

Another idea is to place at each person's seat a 3" x 5" card and pen and have everyone write something for which they are thankful. These can be read during, before, or after the meal.

On another 3" x 5" card have each person write one positive quality about someone else. Examples: "I love you, Uncle Brad, because you make me laugh with your cute jokes," or "I love you, Auntie Christy, because you read to me."

These name cards will give a great opportunity for your family to show God's love, and the Scriptures will put God's Word into the hearts of those who are not in tune with the Lord. The Bible says, "His word will not return void." For 39 years we've been feeding God's Word into my Jewish family through Scripture name cards.

At first they were embarrassed to read them and felt a bit timid, so we would skip those who didn't feel comfortable. But today, 39 years later, the formerly hesitant persons are the ones who ask to read first. I'm excited because I know 39 verses of God's Word have entered their hearts. His Word is sharper than any two-edged sword, and we're trusting God to pierce their hearts with His love. A silent witness can be given in so many ways—especially during the harvest season and on Thanksgiving Day when people are open to talking about being thankful.

## Third Week in November

Use the "Third Week" form at the end of this chapter to make any last-minute arrangements for Thanksgiving. If you'll be going out-of-town, ask a neighbor to collect your mail and newspapers. If you are cooking, finalize your menu and entertainment plans.

---

*A French proverb tells us: "Gratitude is the heart's memory." And so it is. For when we are thankful, we are thinking not only of blessings of the immediate present, but also of good things received in the past. Especially is this so at Thanksgiving*—Esther Burkholder.

---

## Fourth Week in November

I get so excited by this time—and thankful for all I have done and already accomplished toward being ready for Thanksgiving. Use the form at the end of this chapter for your final planning.

Special holiday events will be happening Thanksgiving weekend. Decide which event you want to attend as a family, then schedule one special event for each child individually.

A few days before any holiday meal, I plan and organize my serving dishes. Then I make out 3" x 5" cards, listing on each card what will go into the empty dish, and I place that card in the bowl. That way I don't have to try to remember at the last minute what goes into what. It also makes it easy for guests to help with final preparations.

As you gather around the bountiful table, holding hands can make this a special family and friendship time. Colossians 1:3 says, "We give thanks to God, the Father of our Lord Jesus Christ." Have a beautiful turkey day filled with thanksgiving to God, and don't forget to serve the cranberry sauce or to garnish the platter with parsley.

Now put away the fall decorations and start thinking toward Christmas.

# Blessings Tied to Serving Food

Thanksgiving Day seems to gather from far and wide groups of people, some friends and some strangers, who pause and give thanks for blessings of health, family, job, business, a free country, and the opportunity to worship freely. Thanksgiving for food extends at this festive time to include giving thanks for other blessings. In Deuteronomy 8:10 (NIV) we read, "When you have eaten and are satisfied, praise the LORD your God for the good land he has given you."

---

*Thanksgiving Day comes, by statute, once a year; to the honest man it comes as frequently as the heart of gratitude will allow, which may mean every day, or at least once in seven days*—Edward Sanford Martin.

---

The act of sharing food is mentioned many times in the Gospels—from the plea to "give us this day our daily bread" in the Lord's Prayer to, "While they were eating, Jesus took bread, gave thanks and broke it, and gave it to his disciples, saying, 'Take and eat; this is my body'" (Matthew 26:26 NIV). Even in other cultures and religions around the world, we find blessings tied to the serving of food.

While there was no specific prayer associated with the first Thanksgiving, there were some American Indian blessings found mentioning the sacred gift of food. One of them stated, "If you see no reason for giving thanks, the fault lies in yourself."

The act of saying grace at mealtime gives individuals a sense of a real connection to God. The sense of being close to God can be more powerful than it is with silent prayer. Our grandson Bevan (age 8) always begins his prayers with, "Father God." When he says that, I know that he is approaching God in a very personal way—far beyond my understanding of the divine when I was eight years old.

When someone orally gives a mealtime blessing, there seems to be an instant presence of God that enters into the group. Food prayers offer a simple way to bring expressions of faith into the family unit. Rotate the offer of such prayers to all the members of the family; praying doesn't have to be left up to the man or adult of the home.

In our family, we hold hands around the table, bow our heads, and join together in prayer. Our youngest grandson, Bradley Joe II (2 years old), loves us to end our prayer with the little chorus, "Amen, Amen." Quite often when we visit the Salvation Army, they will collectively sing a hymn or chorus of thanksgiving for their mealtime grace.

If your family isn't used to saying oral prayers of thanksgiving, you might purchase prepared mealtime prayers. Sharing food and prayers of thanksgiving are great ways to draw a family closer to each other and to the Lord. If this isn't already a habit in your family, Thanksgiving Day is a great time to step out and try something new.

---

### Prayers from Around the World

*God most provident, we join all creation in raising to you a hymn of Thanksgiving through Jesus Christ, your Son.*

*For generation upon generation, peoples of this land have sung of your bounty; we too offer you praise for the rich harvest we have received at your hands.Bless us and this food which we share with grateful hearts. . . .*

*Praise and glory to you, Lord God, now and forever.*
> —Traditional Catholic grace

*God,*
*We thank you for all your gifts*
*This day, this night—*

*These fruits, these flowers,*
*These trees, these waters—*
*With all these treasures*
*you have endowed us.*
　　　　—Grace from Pakistan

*Lord, the yam is fat like meat, the cassava melts on the tongue,*
*oranges burst in their peels, dazzling and bright.*

*Lord, nature gives thanks.*

*Your creatures give thanks. Your praise rises in us like the great*
*river.*
　　　　—West African prayer

*A circle of friends is a blessed thing.*
*Sweet is the breaking of bread with friends.*
*For the honor of their presence at our board*
*We are deeply grateful, Lord.*
　　　　—Nineteenth-century American grace[1]

## A Written Prayer for Thanksgiving

*Father God, as I sit down to a Thanksgiving table once*
*again, I want to thank You for Your goodness to me.*

*Thank You for meeting my needs every day—for food and*
*shelter and clothing. And for many extras You provide that*
*I so often take for granted.*

*Thank You for family and friends who make my life com-*
*plete. Thank You that even when we are miles apart, we are*
*bound by the cords of Your love.*

*And I thank You that I live in a country where I am free to*
*worship You and to read Your Word.*

*Most of all, I thank You for Your Son, Jesus Christ, who is the "light of the world." When I turned to Him, He flooded the darkness of my soul with the light of Your love.*

*Thank You that He not only died for my sins, but that He is alive today at Your side—hearing my prayers and preparing a home for me in heaven.*

*Thank You that He came into this world and took up residence in my life as Savior, Lord, and God.*

*Thank You for all that You have given me as a Christian: the Holy Spirit who is Your presence in my life, the Bible that is the light to my pathway, Christian friends who encourage and help me.*

*Thank You that I can face tomorrow with hope because Jesus is living for me.*

*O, Lord, how truly rich I am! Thank You for all You mean to me.*[2]

---

*Be thankful unto him, and bless his name. For the LORD is good; his mercy is everlasting; and his truth endureth to all generations*—Psalm 100:4,5 (KJV).

# Some Extra Thanksgiving Ideas

### ∞ How Much Turkey to Buy

For turkeys 12 pounds or smaller, allow about one pound per person. Larger birds have a higher proportion of meat to bone weight. For a 12- to 24-pound turkey, allow about ¾ pound per person. If you want leftovers, allow 2 pounds per person when buying a turkey 12 pounds or smaller. Allow 1½ pounds per person for 12- to 24-pound birds.

## ∞ Turkey Tips

1. To store a fresh turkey, loosely cover it with waxed paper or foil. Keep the turkey in the coldest part of your refrigerator and cook within three days.

2. You can special-order a turkey from your favorite market. Give them the weight you want and request that it be fresh, not frozen. Pick it up the day before Thanksgiving. You now have a fresh turkey that is ready for the oven.

3. After cooking the turkey, it may be stored three or four days in the refrigerator or frozen and stored up to three months.

4. Keep a frozen turkey in the freezer until you want to cook it. Whole turkeys can be kept frozen for one year, turkey parts for six months.

5. The refrigerator is the best place to thaw your frozen turkey. It keeps meat cold while it defrosts. Allow five hours per pound to thaw.

## ∞ Roasting Time for Turkeys—Oven Temperature 325°F (165°C)

| Size | Stuffed | Unstuffed |
| --- | --- | --- |
| 8–12 pounds | 4–5 hours | 3–4 hours |
| 12–16 pounds | 4½–6 hours | 3½–5 hours |
| 16–20 pounds | 5½–7 hours | 4½–6 hours |
| 20–24 pounds | 6½–7½ hours | 5½–6½ hours |

These times are guidelines only. The meat thermometer should register 185°F (85°C) in the thickest part of the thigh when done.

Juices should run clear when the bird is pierced with a fork between the leg and thigh.

## ∞ *Steps to Standard Turkey Cooking* (Option #1)

1. Wash the turkey well and wipe dry with paper towels. Season the cavity of the bird.

2. Stuff with a favorite dressing.

3. Rub olive oil or Crisco all over the turkey.

4. Use a meat thermometer, if possible, placing it in the thickest part of the thigh and being careful not to hit a bone.

5. Sprinkle with salt and pepper.

6. Place the turkey on a rack in a roasting pan with breast up (however, roasting with the breast down makes a turkey moister).

7. Place aluminum foil over the turkey and pan, with the thermometer sticking out for ease of reading.

8. Place turkey and pan in oven set at 325°F (165°C).

9. Remove the foil from the turkey during the last 30 minutes for final browning.

10. Pour the juices over the bird to assist in the browning process. Be very careful that you don't burn yourself when basting the bird.

11. Let the turkey cool at least 30 to 60 minutes before carving.

## ∞ *Perfect-Every-Time Turkey* (Option #2)

Trust me with this one. I've been making at least four turkeys a year for 40 years, and this recipe from Adelle Davis is the best I have ever found. The white meat will melt in your mouth.

I always used a meat thermometer, so even with this method I still do—just so I know for sure when the turkey's done.

This is a slow-roasting method, but once in the oven, you can forget the turkey until it comes out.

Choose the desired size of turkey, wash it well, and remove the neck and giblets. Dry turkey with paper towels, salt the cavity, and stuff with brown rice dressing or the dressing of your choice. Rub the outside well with pure olive oil.

Put the turkey breast down (this bastes itself, making the white meat very moist) on a poultry rack in a roasting pan uncovered. Put into a 350° preheated oven for one hour to destroy bacteria on the surface. Then adjust the heat to 200° for any size turkey. This is important. The turkey can go in the oven the day before eating it. (Example: I have a 20-pound turkey. At 5:00 P.M. Thanksgiving Eve I put the prepared turkey in the oven at 350° for one hour. I turn the temperature down to 200° and leave the turkey uncovered until it's done the next day about 10:00 or 11:00 A.M.)

Although the cooking times seems startling at first, the meat is amazingly delicious, juicy, and tender. A turkey cooked the regular time at regular temperatures no longer tastes good. And a turkey cooked at this low temperature slices beautifully and shrinks very little. The turkey cannot burn, so it needs no watching, and vitamins and proteins cannot be harmed at such low heat.

A good rule for timing your turkey is to allow about three times longer than moderate-temperature roasting. For example, a 20-pound turkey normally takes 15 minutes per pound to cook and would take five hours. The slow-cook method takes three times five hours so this equals 15 hours of cooking by the slow method. A smaller turkey cooks for 20 minutes per pound, so an 11-pound turkey takes three hours and 40 minutes. Multiplied by three, that equals 11 hours.

Since the lower temperature requires longer cooking, its use must depend on when you wish to serve your turkey. However, once it's done, it will not overcook. You can leave the turkey in an additional three to six hours and it will be perfect. Thus, your roasting can be adjusted entirely to your convenience. Allow yourself plenty of time, and let your meat thermometer be your guide to when the turkey is done. Your only problem could be if you didn't put the turkey in the oven soon enough.

The meat browns perfectly, and you'll get wonderful drippings for gravy.

Try it—everyone will praise you and your turkey.

## ∞ Turkey Carving Tips

Just out of the oven, with juices dripping, the turkey looks and smells wonderful. To graciously serve it from platter to plate, try these carving techniques.

1. Remove the drumstick and thigh by pressing the leg away from the body. The joint connecting the leg to the backbone may snap free. If it doesn't, use a sharp knife and cut the leg from the backbone. Cut dark meat completely from the bone structure by following body contour with a knife.

2. Cut drumsticks and thighs apart by cutting through the joint. It's easy to do if you tilt the drumstick to a convenient angle and slice toward the plate. Place thighs on a separate plate.

3. To slice thigh meat, hold the piece firmly on the plate with a fork. Cut even slices parallel to the bone.

4. Remove half the breast at a time by cutting along the breastbone and rib cage with a sharp knife. Lift meat away from the bone.

5. Place half the breast on a cutting surface and slice evenly against the grain of the meat. Repeat with second half of the breast when additional slices are needed. (An optional method is to turn the bird so you can start with the breast of the turkey and make thin slices. When you have sliced all the meat from one side of the bird, you can rotate the bird so you can slice the other side of the turkey.)

# Other Time-Tested Recipes

## ∞ Chocolate Orange Cheesecake

*Amount:* 6 to 8 servings

1½ cups graham cracker crumbs
2 tablespoons plus ¾ cup sugar
1 tablespoon Pernigotti cocoa, plus additional for dusting top
1 teaspoon ground cinnamon
¼ cup unsalted butter, melted
8 ounces bittersweet chocolate, chopped
½ teaspoon orange oil
1 pound cream cheese at room temperature
½ cup sour cream
5 eggs

Mix graham cracker crumbs with 2 tablespoons sugar, cocoa, and cinnamon. Gradually add melted butter, stirring until crumbs are evenly coated. Press evenly into bottom and two-thirds of the way up the sides of a buttered springform pan that has been covered on the outside with aluminum foil. Refrigerate until ready to fill.

Melt chocolate in double boiler; remove from heat. Place cream cheese in bowl, beat on medium speed until smooth and fluffy (about 10 minutes). Beat in sour cream, ¾ cup sugar, and orange oil. Add eggs, one at a time, beating in between. Beat for 1 to 2 minutes. Using a rubber spatula, gently stir in the chocolate until blended. Stir slowly for 1 to 2 minutes to dispel bubbles.

Pour batter into prepared pan. Bake at 350° until puffed and no longer shiny (35 to 40 minutes). Center will look wet but will firm up when chilled. Transfer to wire rack to cool. When cool, remove foil and sides of pan.

Cover and refrigerate until firm enough to cut easily (4 to 5 hours or overnight). Sift cocoa generously over cake before serving.

## ⊙ Quick and Easy Popovers

*Amount:* 12 muffins or 6 popovers

2 eggs
¼ teaspoon salt
1 cup milk
2 tablespoons unsalted butter, melted
1 cup all-purpose flour

Butter 12 standard-size muffin cups or a popover pan. In a bowl combine eggs and salt. Using a whisk, beat lightly. Stir in milk and butter and beat in the flour until just blended. Do not overbeat. Fill each cup about half full and place in a cold oven. Set temperature to 425° and bake for 25 minutes. Reduce heat to 375° and bake until the popovers are golden (10 to 15 minutes longer). They should be crisp on the outside. Quickly pierce each popover with a thin metal skewer or the tip of a small knife to release the steam. Leave in the oven a couple of minutes for further crisping. Remove and serve at once.

## ⊙ Orange Muffins

*Amount:* 12 standard muffins

⅓ cup dried cranberries, chopped
⅓ cup plus 2 tablespoons sugar
3 tablespoons boiling water
1¾ cups all-purpose flour
½ cup yellow cornmeal
2½ teaspoons baking powder
½ teaspoon baking soda
½ teaspoon salt
2 eggs
1 cup milk
⅓ cup unsalted butter, melted
1 tablespoon grated orange peel

In a small bowl, stir together cranberries and 2 tablespoons sugar. Stir in boiling water; set aside for 15 minutes to soften cranberries. In a large bowl, mix flour, cornmeal, $\frac{1}{3}$ cup sugar, baking powder, baking soda, and salt. In another bowl, using whisk, beat eggs lightly. Add milk and melted butter; beat until smooth. Stir in cranberries, their liquid, and grated orange peel. Stir liquid mixture into flour mixture. Divide batter evenly among buttered muffin cups, filling each ¾ full. Bake at 400° until risen and the tops are golden (15 to 20 minutes). Remove from the oven and let cool in pan for 2 to 3 minutes. Serve warm.

## ∞ Pumpkin Muffins

*Amount:* 10 muffins

½ cup unsalted butter
¼ cup sugar
2 eggs
1⅓ cups all-purpose flour
1 teaspoon baking soda
½ teaspoon salt
1¼ cups Muirhead Pecan-Pumpkin Butter
½ teaspoon pure vanilla extract
2 teaspoons fresh lemon juice
¾ cup currants

In a bowl, beat butter and sugar together until smooth and creamy. Add eggs and beat well. Add flour, baking soda, and salt, and mix until combined. Stir in Pecan-Pumpkin Butter, vanilla extract, lemon juice, and currants. Fill buttered muffin cups ¾ full. Bake in preheated 325° oven until toothpick inserted in center comes out clean (about 25 to 30 minutes). Remove muffins from pan and cool on wire rack.

## ∞ Pumpkin Waffles

*Amount:* 4 servings

½ cup canned pumpkin
1½ cups milk
3 eggs, well beaten
2 tablespoons melted butter
1 cup all-purpose flour, sifted
2 teaspoons baking powder
½ teaspoon salt
2 tablespoons sugar
⅛ teaspoon nutmeg

Stir together pumpkin, eggs, milk, and butter. In a separate bowl, combine flour, baking powder, salt, sugar, and nutmeg. Add dry ingredients to pumpkin mixture. Stir until thoroughly combined. Cook according to the directions for your waffle maker. Serve immediately with berry or maple syrup, fresh berries, or ginger whipped cream.

## ∞ Wild Rice Casserole

*Amount:* 6 servings

1 package (4 ounces) wild and white rice mix
8 ounces bulk pork sausage
1 cup chopped onion
1 cup chopped celery
1 cup shredded fresh spinach
½ cup pitted olives
½ cup reduced-calorie mayonnaise
¾ teaspoon ground sage
½ cup chopped pecans

Prepare rice mix according to package directions. Cook sausage and drain thoroughly.

Cook onion and celery until lightly browned. Add remaining ingredients except pecans. Refrigerate until ready to cook. Preheat oven to 350°. Bake for 30 minutes.

## ∞ Granny's Stuffing

*Amount:* 8 to 10 servings

12 slices white bread, dried
1 medium onion, finely chopped
3 ribs celery, finely chopped
¼ cup chopped parsley
1 teaspoon poultry seasoning
½ teaspoon salt
¼ teaspoon pepper
1 egg, lightly beaten
4 tablespoons melted butter
warm water

Preheat oven to 325°. Break bread into postage-stamp-size pieces in a large bowl. Add onion, celery, and parsley, and mix thoroughly. Sprinkle with poultry seasoning, salt, and pepper, and toss again to mix well. Add egg and mix again. Slowly add warm water, a tablespoon or so at a time, tossing until the bread is very moist, but not dripping, or the stuffing will turn out gummy.

Spoon into greased 8" x 8" casserole. Bake for 30 to 45 minutes.

## ∞ Hot Buttered Cranberry Cider

*Amount:* 10 servings

⅓ cup butter, softened
⅓ cup mild honey
½ teaspoon ginger
½ teaspoon cinnamon

1 48-ounce bottle cranberry juice cocktail
1 quart cider
cinnamon sticks (optional)

Blend softened butter, honey, and spices. This may be done ahead of time.

When ready to serve, combine cranberry cocktail and cider. Bring to a boil or heat in a party percolator. Have butter mixture beside the pot. To serve, put a small spoonful of honey-butter in each mug or heat-proof punch cup. Fill with hot cranberry cider. Stir with a cinnamon stick.

## ∞ Fudgey Pecan Pie

*Amount:* one 9" pie

⅓ cup butter
⅔ cup sugar
⅓ cup cocoa
3 eggs
1 cup light corn syrup
¼ teaspoon salt
1 cup chopped pecans
1 unbaked 9" piecrust
½ cup cold whipping cream
1 tablespoon powdered sugar
¼ teaspoon vanilla extract
pecan halves (optional)

Heat oven to 375°. In a medium saucepan over low heat, melt butter or margarine; add sugar and cocoa, stirring until well blended. Remove from heat, set aside. In medium bowl, beat eggs slightly. Stir in corn syrup and salt. Add cocoa mixture; blend well. Stir in chopped pecans. Pour into unbaked piecrust. Bake in a 375° oven for 45 to 50 minutes or until set. Cool. Cover and let stand 8 hours before serving.

## ‹› Yams in Orange Sauce

*Amount:* 6 to 8 servings

1. Bake 6 medium yams in oven until almost tender (about 45 minutes) at 375° (or bake in microwave at full power for 6 to 8 minutes per pound).

2. Peel and slice potatoes into lightly buttered casserole dish.

3. Blend together and pour over top of potatoes:

   1 cup orange juice
   ¼ cup honey
   2 tablespoons unsalted butter, melted
   2 tablespoons cornstarch

4. Cover and bake at 350° for 30 minutes.

## ‹› Amandine Green Beans

*Amount:* 4 servings

1. Cook green beans whole, or cut diagonally, or French cut lengthwise, as desired:

   ⅔ to 1 pound fresh green beans (or 10-ounce package, frozen)

2. Sauté almonds in butter until lightly golden brown and fold in hot cooked beans:

   1 tablespoon melted butter
   ¼ cup slivered or sliced almonds

# Those Yummy Leftovers

After looking at that turkey carcass all day, your first inclination is to give it away or throw it away—anything to just get rid of it. But don't. This is the best way to be creative and a great money-saver.

Gently place before one of the men or older boys of the group the carcass on a tray and request them to cut away all the turkey still remaining, and to leave just the bones. As the dishes are being washed by someone, you can be placing a picked-clean carcass in a soup pot.

In about two hours, you'll have delicious stock that can be frozen for soup or prepared the next day. Now you can throw out the carcass. (Be sure to keep it away from family pets. The bones splinter and can get lodged in your pet's throat.)

If after dinner you just can't face that carcass one more minute, put it in a plastic bag and store it in the refrigerator until after breakfast the next day.

## ෨ Turkey Soup Stock

enough water to cover the carcass (8 to 10 cups)
turkey carcass, broken
any leftover pan juices or gravy
1 onion, quartered
2 large cloves of garlic, whole but peeled and slightly smashed
1 carrot, cut into large pieces
4 to 5 stalks celery, with tops and leaves, cut into large pieces
1 teaspoon dried marjoram
1 teaspoon dried thyme (or fresh sprigs)
½ teaspoon dried sage (or fresh sprigs)
a few sprigs fresh parsley
½ teaspoon salt
½ teaspoon cayenne pepper
freshly ground pepper

In a large pot bring the water to a boil. Add all ingredients. Reduce heat to a low simmer. Cover and simmer for two hours. Remove from heat.

When cool enough, pick out any meat that has fallen off the bones to add later to the soup. Strain, pour into a freezer container, and refrigerate. Once it has cooled, freeze stock or keep refrigerated until ready to make soup. (The fat will rise to the top and make a seal. Remove it when ready to make soup.)

If using fresh beans in the soup, place 1 cup dry beans in 3 cups water in a covered saucepan. Simmer one hour or until tender while stock is cooking. This yields about two cups cooked beans.

## ∞ Turkey Soup

1 large onion, finely chopped
1 teaspoon olive oil
8 cups turkey or chicken stock (fresh or canned)
1½ cups carrots, sliced into thin circles
1½ cups celery, diced
3 turnips or small rutabagas, halved and sliced thin
3 medium red- or white-skinned potatoes, quartered and
    sliced thin
1 cup navy or northern (white) beans—fresh, soaked,
    and cooked or canned, rinsed, and drained
2 to 3 cups leftover turkey, cut into bite-sized pieces
1 to 2 cups leftover cooked green beans
cauliflower (optional)
fresh parsley, finely chopped
parmesan cheese, freshly grated

Using a large pot, sauté onion in oil until limp. Pour in stock and add the rest of the ingredients, including fresh cooked beans (but not canned beans). Don't add the leftover vegetables, parsley, and cheese yet. Cover and simmer for about 30 minutes.

Check to see if the vegetables are tender. Simmer longer, if needed.

When soup is done, add canned beans (if used) and leftover cooked vegetables. Top with grated cheese and chopped parsley.

## ∞ Turkey Hash

> 6 medium red- or white-skinned potatoes, cut into
>     ½-inch cubes (about 3 cups)
> ½ cup turkey or chicken broth (fresh or canned)
> 1 medium onion, chopped
> 2 stalks celery, finely chopped (about 1 cup)
> 1 large clove garlic, minced
> 1 sweet red pepper, chopped
> 2 cups cooked turkey, chopped into small pieces
> ⅛ teaspoon nutmeg
> ½ teaspoon sage
> ½ teaspoon thyme
> ½ teaspoon cayenne pepper
> salt
> freshly ground pepper
> fresh paprika
> parsley, minced (optional)

Put potatoes and broth in a 12-inch skillet (preferably nonstick). Cover and simmer for 15 minutes until broth has evaporated and potatoes are tender and lightly browned on one side. Add onion, celery, and garlic and sauté for a few minutes over medium heat, stirring occasionally.

Add the rest of the ingredients, with the exception of the paprika and parsley. Let cook for a few minutes on one side, then flip over in sections. Don't overstir. Add a little oil if pan is too dry.

When celery is tender and hash is browned, serve sprinkled with parsley and paprika.

## ∞ Mashed Potato Pancakes

*Amount:* 4 servings

> 1 clove garlic, minced
> ½ teaspoon jalapeño pepper, minced

canola oil
2 green onions, finely chopped
2 cups leftover mashed potatoes
1 egg, beaten, or 1 egg white

In nonstick skillet (10- to 12-inch), sauté garlic and hot pepper in a few drops of oil for a minute. Stir in green onions for a few seconds; remove from heat. In a mixing bowl, stir together all the ingredients.

Heat a little oil in a skillet. Drop batter into the pan by spoonfuls, making small 2-inch cakes. Flatten with a spatula, and fry on medium-high heat for approximately 2 minutes per side. Flip over when bottom is brown. Serve with low-fat sour cream or yogurt.

## ∞ Mediterranean Noodle Turkey Casserole

*Amount:* 8 servings

1 pound medium egg noodles, uncooked
14½-ounce can low-sodium chicken broth
1 cup skim milk
1 teaspoon salt
¼ cup cornstarch
2 cups chopped, cooked turkey
14-ounce can artichoke hearts, drained and quartered
17½-ounce jar roasted red peppers, drained and sliced
9 Calamata olives, pitted and sliced
½ cup grated part-skim mozzarella cheese
½ cup white wine
1 teaspoon lemon juice
½ teaspoon black pepper
vegetable-oil cooking spray
2 tablespoons grated parmesan cheese

Prepare noodles according to package directions. Drain.

Stir the broth, milk, salt, and cornstarch together in a large pot or Dutch oven until the cornstarch is dissolved. Cook over medium heat, stirring constantly, until thickened and bubbly. Stir in noodles, turkey, artichoke hearts, red peppers, olives, mozzarella cheese, wine, lemon juice, and black pepper.

Spray a 3-quart baking dish with cooking spray. Spoon noodle mixture into dish. Sprinkle with parmesan cheese. Bake in a 350° oven for about 35 minutes. Let stand 5 minutes before serving.

## Other Helpful Thanksgiving Ideas

1. *Chopped onion without tears*—Take the tears out of preparing onions by chopping them in a blender. Cut an onion in quarters or eighths. Fill the blender halfway with water. Add onion pieces. Push the chop button on and off until the onion is chopped to the desired size. Drain onions in a colander. Repeat until you have enough onions for your recipe.

2. *Orange shells*—This is a simple, decorative way to serve your sweet potatoes or yams. Cut oranges in half and remove fruit and pulp. Add the fruit to your holiday punch. Prepare cooked yams or sweet potatoes and spoon into the orange shells. Nestle oranges around turkey on platter. For an extra touch, flute top edges of orange shells with a knife and top with a maraschino cherry (or top with a small marshmallow and place them in the oven until the marshmallow melts).

3. *Unconventional day*—Your family may want to plan a day very different from the traditional family gathering. Your plans might include a trip to the beach (climate permitting), the park, the mountains, or the desert. You might even have hamburgers and hot dogs. Be sure to bring along some thoughts of inspiration to share together.

4. *Rent a cabin*—You might consider renting a cabin for the four-day holiday and invite friends and family to share this special

period of time with you. Have each family bring their own bedding and supply meals for one day. In the evening you can spend time getting started on some Christmas decorations—a great way to cement family relationships.

---

*Heap high the board with plenteous cheer, and gather to the feast, and toast the sturdy Pilgrim band whose courage never ceased—*Alice W. Brotherton, *The First Thanksgiving.*

---

5. *Hostess gifts*—If you are going to be a guest in someone's home, plan to take an inexpensive hostess gift. A plate of homemade cookies, stationery, tea towels with a bow tied around them, or even a new turkey baster would be appreciated.

6. *Ask children to help*—This is a great time to include the children in the kitchen. They can help scrub vegetables, dry off lettuce, stir whipped cream, set the table, place ice cubes in drinks, etc. This makes them feel a part of the festivities.

7. *Have a potluck*—If you find yourself too busy to do all the cooking, decide to make your harvest dinner a potluck. Call the guests and assign them each a dish to bring.

8. *Pick chores*—As your guests arrive, have them draw out of a hat a slip of paper that will give them a chore for the day. The slips might read:

   ◆ Mash the potatoes.
   ◆ Make giblet gravy.
   ◆ Put ice cubes in the glasses.

9. *Make "thankful cards"*—Have someone make out a card for each person titled, "I'm thankful for . . ." After dinner, each guest will read a thankful card. This is a great way to focus on the positive

things God provides to us. Or you could have a person interview each guest asking the question, "What is the best thing that has happened to you this year, month, week, or today?" This exercise has given us many great times of communication and has brought tears to each of us.

---

*Be joyful always; pray continually; give thanks in all circumstances, for this is God's will for you in Christ Jesus*—1 Thessalonians 5:16-18 (NIV).

---

10. *Make Scripture name cards*—Assign to one of the children or to your husband the task of making individual name cards with a Scripture verse on the back. These verses should be in line with Thanksgiving. (Example: Romans 5:20, "Always give thanks for all things in the name of our Lord Jesus Christ.") You can use 3" x 5" cards folded in half, placing the name on the front and the Scripture inside. These will be read by each person as the blessing of thanks before your meal.

11. *Design a centerpiece*—A few days before Thanksgiving, set the table. Make it simple. Use a pumpkin and some fresh fruit around it for a centerpiece. Include three candles in an autumn color using different designed holders (or use votive candles and float them in a glass or bowl of water). Try to use items you already have.

---

*Let us come before him with thanksgiving and extol him with music and song*—Psalm 95:2 (NIV).

---

# ᔓCalendarᔕ

Month ____ Year ____

| | | | | |
|---|---|---|---|---|
| ☐ | ☐ | ☐ | ☐ | ☐ |
| ☐ | ☐ | ☐ | ☐ | ☐ |
| ☐ | ☐ | ☐ | ☐ | ☐ |
| ☐ | ☐ | ☐ | ☐ | ☐ |
| ☐ | ☐ | ☐ | ☐ | ☐ |
| ☐ | ☐ | ☐ | ☐ | ☐ |
| ☐ | ☐ | ☐ | ☐ | ☐ |

# November: Week 1—Things to Do

Activity                                                    Done (x)

1._____ ☐

2._____ ☐

3._____ ☐

4._____ ☐

5._____ ☐

6._____ ☐

7._____ ☐

8._____ ☐

9._____ ☐

11._____ ☐

12._____ ☐

13._____ ☐

14._____ ☐

15._____ ☐

# November: Week 2—Things to Do

| Activity | Done (x) |
|---|---|
| 1._____ | □ |
| 2._____ | □ |
| 3._____ | □ |
| 4._____ | □ |
| 5._____ | □ |
| 6._____ | □ |
| 7._____ | □ |
| 8._____ | □ |
| 9._____ | □ |
| 11._____ | □ |
| 12._____ | □ |
| 13._____ | □ |
| 14._____ | □ |
| 15._____ | □ |

# November: Week 3—Things to Do

Activity                                                    Done (x)

1._____ □

2._____ □

3._____ □

4._____ □

5._____ □

6._____ □

7._____ □

8._____ □

9._____ □

11._____ □

12._____ □

13._____ □

14._____ □

15._____ □

# November: Week 4—Things to Do

| Activity | Done (x) |
|---|---|
| 1._____ | ☐ |
| 2._____ | ☐ |
| 3._____ | ☐ |
| 4._____ | ☐ |
| 5._____ | ☐ |
| 6._____ | ☐ |
| 7._____ | ☐ |
| 8._____ | ☐ |
| 9._____ | ☐ |
| 11._____ | ☐ |
| 12._____ | ☐ |
| 13._____ | ☐ |
| 14._____ | ☐ |
| 15._____ | ☐ |

# 9

## Hanukkah

*"I AM THE LIGHT* of the world; he who follows Me shall not walk in the darkness, but shall have the light of life" (John 8:12).

**When Observed:** Celebrated for eight days, beginning the twenty-fifth day of the Hebrew month Kislev (November-December)

**Earliest Observance:** 165 B.C. in Jerusalem

My background being Jewish, I find it only fitting to share what at one time was a very important part of my childhood: Hanukkah or Chanukah—either spelling is correct.

Many Gentiles today do not know what the story of Hanukkah is all about. Perhaps you have Jewish friends or your children have friends at school who practice the Jewish faith. It's a wonderful learning experience to know why and what people are talking about when they say, "I'm Jewish and we celebrate Hanukkah."

## An Eternal Feast of Light

Hanukkah is the commemoration of a miracle whose story has fascinated and inspired generation after generation of Jewish people.

Over 20 centuries ago, the land of Judea was under the rule of a Syrian king. For a time, the Jews of Judea were free to practice their customs and observe the laws of the Torah—that is, until the reign of King Antiochus.

Antiochus was determined that all those under his rule believe in the multigod religion of the Greeks, as he did. He sent men to Judea to enforce his command and sent soldiers to the temple in Jerusalem. They burned the Torah scrolls. They ripped the curtains and smashed the beautiful menorah. A Greek idol replaced these things on the temple altar. No longer could the Jews worship in their temple, and some gave in to the king's command to worship other gods.

Near Jerusalem in the town of Modi'in, the leader of the town, Mattathias, rebelled against the king and led many of the townspeople away to the mountains where they hid and organized a small army to fight the Syrians. Mattathias, however, was old and in poor health. Before long, he realized that he would not survive to lead his army. Judah, one of his five sons, was appointed as leader and was given the name Maccabee. His army became known as the Maccabees.

They lacked numbers, experience, and weaponry, but they knew the terrain and were able to surprise the king's soldiers several times. More importantly, they were fighting with God for the freedom to practice their faith.

After three years of fighting, they reached Jerusalem and went to the temple. They found it desecrated and in a state of shambles. The fighters became builders and, after much hard labor, the temple was again ready for worship. On the twenty-fifth day of the month of Kislev on the Jewish calendar, the great menorah was ready to be lit. But only specially purified oil could be used, and there was none to be found. A massive search finally yielded only a day's supply. More oil would have to be obtained from the town of Tekoah, but even using the best horse and fastest rider, it would take eight days to obtain. Nevertheless, the menorah was lit with the knowledge that the temple would soon be in darkness again until the rider returned with more oil.

The next day, the high priest entered the temple. To his amazement, the menorah was still burning. This continued for eight days until the rider returned with the necessary oil. Before long, everyone had heard about the great miracle. God had provided the light! Man's best efforts would have left him in darkness, but God provided the light.

Menorahs will burn for eight days in countless Jewish homes to commemorate and celebrate Hanukkah, the "feast of light." The prophet Isaiah, however, foresaw an even greater miracle of light that was to occur. He proclaimed:

> The people who walk in darkness will see a great light; those who live in a dark land, the light will shine on them. . . . For a child will be born to us, a son will be given to us; and the government will rest on His shoulders; and His name will be called Wonderful Counselor, Mighty God, Eternal Father, Prince of Peace. There will be no end to the increase of His government or of peace (Isaiah 9:2,6,7).

Of course, this passage speaks of the coming of the promised Messiah of Israel. Many Jews anticipate this as a future event. Many more speak of "when the Messiah comes" as more of a joke or legend than an anticipation. But Isaiah foresaw this, too, and wrote:

> "Keep on listening, but do not perceive; keep on looking, but do not understand." Render the heart of this people insensitive, their ears dull, and their eyes dim, lest they see with their eyes, hear with their ears, understand with their hearts, and return and be healed (Isaiah 6:9,10).

The prophet also foresaw that the Messiah, the Great Light, would be rejected by His own people because of their blindness:

> Who has believed our message? And to whom has
> the arm of the LORD been revealed? For He grew up
> before Him like a tender shoot, and like a root out of
> parched ground; He has no stately form or majesty that
> we should look upon Him, nor appearance that we should
> be attracted to Him. He was despised and forsaken of
> men, a man of sorrows, and acquainted with grief; and
> like one from whom men hide their face, He was de-
> spised, and we did not esteem Him (Isaiah 53:1-3).

But Isaiah did say that at least some of the people would see the great light about which he had prophesied. God is able to open the eyes of the blind. So it was that some seven centuries after Isaiah's prophecy, a Jewish man by the name of Jochanan (better known by his Greek name John) was able to proclaim about another Jewish man: "In Him was life, and the life was the light of men" (John 1:4). He was speaking of Yeshua (Jesus) of Nazareth.

It didn't stop with John. For nearly 2000 years now, there has always been a small pocket of Jewish people who have accepted that Jesus—who fulfilled all of Isaiah's messianic prophecies and hundreds of other Old Testament messianic prophecies—is the great light that God promised. True, the majority of the Jewish community rejects this idea, but didn't Isaiah say this would be the case?

Hanukkah is the celebration of God's miraculous provision of light. The best efforts of man would have left him in darkness, but God provided the light. So it is with the Messiah. Our own best efforts in life still leave us uncertain and without peace concerning our origin, purpose, or final destiny. Man has accomplished many things but, to the extent that we are unable to understand the above three issues, we walk in darkness. This very darkness, Isaiah proclaimed, was to be illumined by the Messiah.

Has this happened to you? Is your "feast of light" only eight days long, or do you walk in light all year? Do you understand where you came from, why you are here, and where you are going, or are you still one of "the people who walk in darkness"?

John, the New Testament writer, made this assessment concerning the "light of men" he saw in Jesus: "And the light shines in the darkness, and the darkness did not comprehend it" (John 1:5). His words sounds an awful lot like Isaiah's, don't they?

There will be two celebrations in December that won't be all they should be. One will be the celebration of Christmas as a day of presents and Santa Claus. The other will be the celebration for only eight days of God's provision of light. Hanukkah commemorates a wonderful miracle, and it should be celebrated. But wouldn't it be tragic to celebrate only the eight-day feast of light and remain blind to the fact that God, through His Son, the Messiah, has provided the greatest miracle—an eternal feast of light just for the asking? We need to open our eyes—a great light is shining brightly!

Hanukkah and all its food traditions emphasize oil—including the preparation of *latkes*, or potato pancakes, which are served for this holiday around the world.

Ashkenazic Jews from Germany and Eastern Europe celebrate Hanukkah by frying what have become traditional latkes for most Americans. Sephardic Jews, originally from Spain, emigrated to most countries around the Mediterranean, and they, too, prepare versions of fried potato pancakes to mark the occasion.

The food processor is a must for making East European latkes— no more hand grating the potatoes. The food processor has sped up latke preparation so much that the potatoes don't have time to turn dark.

French *galettes*—crisp, golden pancakes made from shredded potatoes—are another variation on traditional latkes. The key to making the best galettes is baking the potatoes before shredding them. Unfortunately, these potatoes still require hand-grating because they become gluey in the food processor. On the other hand, this is one latke you can brown in advance and recrisp in a hot oven at party time.

*Gnocchi*, Italian potato dumplings, offer another opportunity for advance preparation. After you shape and boil the gnocchi, you can set them aside until almost serving time, then heat them in the oven and serve with any number of sauces. Marinara, Gorgonzola, and pesto sauces each enhance the flavor of gnocchi. If you don't want to bother with a sauce, sprinkle them with freshly grated parmesan cheese.

Gnocchi preparation has inspired intense debate. Some cooks favor including egg yolks, saying they make the dough easier to handle. Others argue against the yolks, saying the finished dumpling is much lighter without them.

In India, hot mashed potatoes are shaped into patties and fried. Seasoned with onions, ginger, bell peppers, and chopped cashews, these *aloo vadai* are a spicy way to celebrate Hanukkah, and you can make the batter and shape the patties in advance. At party time, all you have to do is fry and serve them.

You can even make potato pancakes from sweet potatoes. This popular North African-style recipe is eaten with a hot pepper sauce, such as Tabasco, and a cooling yogurt-and-cucumber raita. Preparation is easy because the food processor does the grating. To make party preparation easier, refrigerate the batter up to four hours before frying the pancakes.

## ∞ Raita

2 cups yogurt
1 cucumber
3 teaspoons cumin
½ teaspoon salt
pinch of black pepper
pinch of cayenne pepper (or dash of Tabasco sauce)
chopped parsley

Mix the yogurt and cucumber together and place in the refrigerator for 30 minutes.

Add the other ingredients before serving and garnish with parsley.

# Hanukkah Traditions

One of the best parts of this season is the food, especially the latkes. They are crisp and brown and served with homemade applesauce, sour cream, or yogurt.

*Latke* is a Russian word, meaning "flat cake." Making latkes was adopted because the Jews wanted to serve a dish cooked in oil to symbolize the miracle of Hanukkah.

The symbolism behind the pancakes is threefold. Made initially of flour and water, they served as a reminder of the food hurriedly prepared for the troops as they went to war. The oil used to prepare the pancakes symbolizes the oil that burned for eight days. The eating of latkes commemorates the liberation from Greek rule.

During the eight days of Hanukkah, latkes are eaten daily. They are a delicacy and quite versatile. They can be served for breakfast, brunch, lunch, dinner, or even as a snack. Plain or fancy, they can be eaten with sugar, yogurt, applesauce, or chicken soup. They can be made with buckwheat or potatoes.

It might be fun to have a Hanukkah party for your family, serve latkes and homemade applesauce, and tell the story of Hanukkah. Perhaps you can have candles available or borrow a menorah and show how one candle is lit for every day of Hanukkah. This could be done in an adult Sunday school class, also.

## ‌ Traditional Potato Latkes

*Amount:* 26 pancakes

6 medium potatoes (about 2½ pounds), washed
    thoroughly and cubed
½ medium onion
3 tablespoons flour
2 eggs
1½ teaspoons salt or to taste
¼ teaspoon freshly ground pepper
oil for frying

Mix all ingredients except oil. Place ¼ of the mixture in a food processor and process until coarsely chopped. Repeat until all the ingredients are combined. Work quickly so mixture does not darken.

Heat a scant tablespoon of oil in a nonstick skillet. Cover the bottom evenly. Use a ¼-cup measure to pour the potato batter into the heated skillet and form patties. Fry until crisp and brown; turn and repeat. Drain on paper towels to remove excess oil. Keep latkes warm until all the batter is fried.

## ෨ French Potato Galettes

*Amount:* 22 pancakes

> 6 medium baking potatoes (about 2½ pounds), washed
> salt and pepper to taste
> 2 eggs, slightly beaten
> oil for frying

Preheat oven to 400°. Bake potatoes 1 hour. Allow them to cool thoroughly.

Peel cold potatoes. Grate through a grater with large holes. Season to taste with salt and pepper. Add eggs. Toss lightly.

Heat enough oil to cover the bottom of a nonstick skillet. Using a ¼-cup measure, ladle potato mixture to form patties in skillet. Do not crowd. Cook over medium-high heat until pancakes are brown and crisp; turn and repeat. Keep latkes warm while preparing the rest of the batter. Repeat until all the batter is fried.

To make ahead, brown the potato pancakes and set aside. Keep at room temperature. Recrisp by heating in 425° oven.

## ෨ Indian Potato Patties (Aloo Vadai)

> 2 large sweet potatoes (about 1 pound), washed and
>    cut into pieces
> 1½ teaspoons salt, or to taste
> ½ teaspoon white pepper

5 eggs, slightly beaten
oil for frying

Grate the potatoes in the food processor, using the blade with large holes. Place in a medium mixing bowl and toss with remaining ingredients except oil. Mix well. Cover and refrigerate (up to 4 hours) until frying time.

Heat enough oil to cover the bottom of a large nonstick skillet. Using a ¼-cup measure, ladle into skillet to form patties, but don't crowd. Cook until crisp and brown on one side; turn and repeat. Keep patties warm while cooking remaining batter.

## ∞ *Emilie's Favorite Applesauce*

*Amount:* 3 cups

1½ pounds of tart baking apples (a mixture of different
    kinds is ideal)
½ teaspoon cinnamon or to taste
¼ teaspoon nutmeg or to taste
½ cup apple juice, apple cider, pineapple juice, or water
1 slice lemon

Wash apples but do not peel. Cut up washed apples and place in a pot. Add fruit juice or cider and spices. If you like a thinner sauce, add a little more fruit juice. Bring to a boil; then reduce heat and simmer for about 10 minutes. Cool; then mix in blender for the best applesauce you have ever tasted. This recipe can be done in a microwave on high for about 5 minutes. If you don't want to use the blender, cook longer until mushy, and then whip with a fork. If you use a Crockpot, cook on low for 4 to 6 hours or until apples fall apart. Whip with a fork.

# Other Hanukkah Foods

## ∽ Holiday Borscht

*Amount:* 15 cups (12 first-course servings)

    3 bunches medium-size beets (about 2 pounds beets
        without leaves)
    3 medium-size onions
    1 tablespoon salad oil
    3 extra-large vegetable bouillon cubes (or 6 envelopes of
        instant vegetable broth and seasoning)
    4 large carrots (about ¾ pound)
    6 medium-size potatoes (about 2 pounds)
    ¼ cup lemon juice
    3 tablespoons sugar
    1 teaspoon salt

*About 2½ hours before serving or one day ahead:*

1. Cut off stems and leaves from beets. Reserve beet greens for use in slaw recipe. Rinse beets with cold running water. Peel and cut beets into ¼-inch pieces.

2. Slice onions thinly. In 5-quart Dutch oven over medium-high heat, cook onions in hot salad oil until golden, stirring occasionally (about 10 minutes). Stir in beets, bouillon, and 2½ quarts water. Increase heat to high; heat to boiling. Reduce heat to low; cover and simmer 30 minutes.

3. Meanwhile, peel and shred carrots coarsely. Stir carrots into beet mixture; simmer 15 minutes longer or until beets and carrots are tender. If not serving on the same day, cover and refrigerate soup.

*About 1 hour before serving:*

4. In 3-quart saucepan over high heat, heat potatoes and enough

water to cover them to boiling. Reduce heat to low. Cover and simmer 25 to 30 minutes until potatoes are fork-tender. Drain potatoes; cool until easy to handle.

5. To serve, peel and dice potatoes. Add lemon juice, sugar, and salt to borscht; heat through. Place diced potatoes in soup bowls and top with borscht.

## ∽ Sweet and Sour Brisket

*Amount:* 12 main-dish servings

 1 4½-pound beef brisket
 1 tablespoon salad oil
 2 12-ounce jars apricot jam
 ½ cup chili sauce
 ¼ cup cider vinegar
 1 tablespoon dry mustard
 1 teaspoon salt
 2 8-ounce packages dried mixed fruit

*About 4 hours before serving:*

1. Trim excess fat from beef brisket. In 8-quart Dutch oven over medium-high heat, cook brisket in hot salad oil until well browned on both sides.

2. Add 4 cups water to brisket in Dutch oven; heat to boiling. Reduce heat to low; cover and simmer 2½ hours or until meat is fork-tender.

3. When brisket is done, preheat oven to 375°. In 3-quart saucepan, combine apricot jam, chili sauce, vinegar, mustard, and salt over medium heat. Heat until jam melts.

4. Line medium roasting pan (about 14" x 10") with foil. Place brisket in pan; reserve cooking fluid. Spread ¾ cup apricot-jam mixture on top of brisket. Bake brisket about 25 minutes or until glaze is lightly browned.

5. Meanwhile, add dried fruit and 2 cups remaining apricot-jam mixture to saucepan. Over high heat, heat to boiling. Reduce heat to low; cover and simmer 20 minutes or until fruit is tender.

6. Slice brisket across the grain and serve with warm fruit sauce.

## ෨ Cabbage and Beet-Green Slaw

*Amount:* 12 servings

    1 medium-size head green cabbage (2 pounds)
    1 medium-size head red cabbage (2 pounds)
    1 medium-size red onion
    ¾ cup mayonnaise
    ¼ cup cider vinegar
    2 tablespoons Dijon mustard
    1 teaspoon salt
    ½ teaspoon coarsely ground black pepper
    3 cups loosely packed beet leaves or spinach leaves

*About 4 hours before serving or early in day:*

1. Thinly slice both kinds of cabbage and discard tough ribs; place in large bowl. Cut onion in half lengthwise, then cut each half crosswise into paper-thin slices. Add onion to cabbage.

2. In small bowl, with wire whisk or fork, mix mayonnaise, vinegar, sugar, mustard, salt, and pepper. Add to cabbage mixture and toss to coat well. Cover bowl with plastic wrap and refrigerate at least 3 hours before serving to allow flavors to blend.

3. Meanwhile, rinse beet leaves with cold running water and pat dry with paper towels. Cut beet leaves into julienne strips; cover with plastic wrap and refrigerate until ready to serve salad.

4. To serve, toss julienne beet leaves with cabbage mixture.

## ∞ Apple and Pear Baskets

*Amount:* 12 servings

12 sheets fresh or frozen (thawed) phyllo (about half of
   a 16-ounce package)
margarine
7 medium-size Golden Delicious apples (about 3½ pounds)
brown sugar
lemon juice
7 medium-size Bartlett pears (about 3½ pounds)
½ cup dried cherries or raisins
2 pints vanilla frozen nondairy dessert

*About 3 hours before serving or day ahead:*

1. Preheat oven to 375°. On work surface, stack sheets of phyllo
(about 17" by 12" each), one on top of the other. With knife, cut
stack lengthwise in half, then crosswise in half (you will have 48
8½" by 6" sheets of phyllo).

2. In small saucepan over low heat, melt 4 tablespoons margarine
(½ stick).

3. Lightly brush 6 10-ounce custard cups with melted margarine.
Place 2 sheets of phyllo, one on top of the other; brush top sheet
with some melted margarine. Arrange phyllo in a custard cup.
Place 2 more sheets of phyllo, one on top of the other, and brush
top sheet with some melted margarine and place crosswise over
phyllo in cup. Crimp edges of phyllo to make a pretty edge. Repeat with 20 more phyllo sheets to make 5 more cups. Keep remaining phyllo covered with damp towels to prevent it from
drying out.

4. Place custard cups in jelly-roll pan for easier handling. Bake
phyllo cups 10 to 12 minutes until phyllo is crisp and golden.
Cool in cups on wire racks about 15 minutes, then carefully remove phyllo cups from custard cups.

5. Repeat with remaining phyllo and melted margarine to make 6 more phyllo cups. If not serving right away, store phyllo cups in tightly covered container or zippered plastic bags until ready to use.

6. Peel and slice apples. In 12-inch skillet over high heat, heat 3 tablespoons margarine, 3 tablespoons packed brown sugar, and 1 teaspoon lemon juice until melted. Stir in the apples to coat them. Continue cooking over high heat until apples are golden brown and softened (about 15 minutes). Remove apples to a bowl.

7. Peel and slice pears. In same skillet over high heat, cook 3 tablespoons margarine, 3 tablespoons brown sugar, and 1 teaspoon lemon juice until melted. Stir in pears and dried cherries to coat them. Continue cooking over high heat until pears are golden and liquid thickens (about 20 minutes). Add pears to apple mixture in bowl. If not serving right away, cover and refrigerate.

8. To serve, reheat fruit mixture. Arrange phyllo cups on platter. Place scoop of frozen nondairy dessert in each phyllo cup; top with warm fruit. Serve immediately.

## ∞ Surprise Hanukkah Gelt

*Amount:* 24 candies

    2 4-ounce packages sweet cooking chocolate
    2 1-ounce squares unsweetened chocolate
    ¼ of 12-ounce bag of pretzels
    24 gold and/or silver foil squares (4" by 4") (available wherever chocolate and candy-making supplies are sold)

*About 1½ hours before serving or up to 1 week ahead:*

1. Place a 16-inch-long piece of plastic wrap over top of mini muffin pan (with 12 1¾-inch cups); press plastic wrap into each cup. Repeat with a second pan. Set pans aside.

2. Chop both kinds of chocolate and place in heavy 2-quart saucepan. Over low heat, cook chocolate, stirring frequently, until melted and smooth. Remove saucepan from heat.

3. Place pretzels in heavyweight plastic bag. Crush pretzels lightly with rolling pin; stir into melted chocolate.

4. Spoon chocolate mixture into mini muffin-pan cups to fill almost halfway, or place chocolate mixture in a heavyweight plastic bag. With scissors, snip off one corner of bag and squeeze chocolate mixture into mini muffin-pan cups. Gently tap muffin pans on counter to distribute chocolate mixture evenly. Refrigerate 30 minutes or until chocolate is firm and fully set.

5. Remove pans from refrigerator. Peel plastic wrap from chocolates and trim any rough edges with knife. Wrap each chocolate in a gold or silver foil square.

---

*You are the light of the world. A city on a hill cannot be hidden. Neither do people light a lamp and put it under a bowl. Instead they put it on its stand, and it gives light to everyone in the house. In the same way, let your light shine before men, that they may see your good deeds and praise your Father in heaven*—Matthew 5:14-16 (NIV).

# 10

*Christmas*

"FOR TODAY IN THE CITY of David there has been born for you a Savior, who is Christ the Lord (Luke 2:11).

**When Observed:** December 25
**Earliest Observance:** Early fourth century

Once a year the Christmas season influences both the sacred and secular segments of life. Christmas is everywhere: on the side of buses, in malls, on banners, in music on the radio and television, and in CD music in our living rooms. For approximately 45 days each year our culture confronts Jesus.

You may accept Him or reject Him, but you can't ignore Him because He's everywhere.

For those of us who claim His name, Christmas ushers in a wonderful time of the year. This season speaks of the Truth. Because of God's gift of His Son born in Bethlehem, nothing can separate us from His love. Light, life, and love are again on our side. The world pauses to listen.

We, as Christians, should be witnesses telling others whereby they, too, can find hope, joy, and strength in their lives.

We must be transformed by His grace—not through our efforts but by what Christ did in His birth, life, and death on the cross.

This grace and future hope can be experienced here on earth

in the present time. In John 10:10 (NIV), Jesus said, "I have come that they may have life, and have it to the full."

Christmas is the good news of transforming grace. Through Jesus Christ we are freed to take on a life of new meaning—a life that is trusting, hopeful, and compassionate.

Christmas reminds us of why we are here, and the "why" questions of life are often the most important ones we ask. Without that understanding, we just go through the agonizing motions of the world, not realizing or recognizing the significance of this season.

Christmas celebrates the birth of Jesus Christ with the message of peace on earth, goodwill toward men. Luke 2:1-7 says:

> Now it came about in those days that a decree went out from Caesar Augustus, that a census be taken of all the inhabited earth. This was the first census taken while Quirinius was governor of Syria. And all were proceeding to register for the census, everyone to his own city. And Joseph also went up from Galilee, from the city of Nazareth, to Judea, to the city of David, which is called Bethlehem, because he was of the house and family of David, in order to register, along with Mary, who was engaged to him, and was with child. And it came about that while they were there, the days were completed for her to give birth. And she gave birth to her first-born son; and she wrapped Him in cloths, and laid Him in a manger, because there was no room for them in the inn.

Although the commercialization of Christmas is frustrating to many people, the celebration can give a warm glow at a cold time of the year.

People in a hundred languages sing the joys of Christmas and share their respective countries' traditions. Austria gave us "Silent Night"; England contributed the mistletoe ball and wassail; Germany, the Christmas tree; Scandinavia, the Yule candle and Yule log; Mexico, the poinsettia plant. These traditions continue to be celebrated with fresh and innovative ideas.

The biblical narrative of the birth of Jesus contains no indication of the date that the event occurred. Luke's report, however, that the shepherds were "staying out in the fields, and keeping watch over their flock by night," suggests that Jesus may have been born in summer or early fall.

---

### Jesus

*The Word of God became flesh . . .*
*The Son of God became man . . .*
*The Lord of all became a servant . . .*
*The Righteous One was made sin . . .*
*The Eternal One tasted death . . .*
*The Risen One now lives in men . . .*
*The Seated One is coming again!*

In the third century, efforts were made to determine the actual date of the nativity, but only in a.d. 336 was definite mention made of December 25.

The early Puritans in America felt that they could not celebrate this day for which there was no biblical sanction. Generally speaking, feelings toward Christmas were divided according to religious denomination.

The diminishing objection to Christmas after 1750 was brought about by the rapid growth of America as a whole. In 1836, Alabama was the first state to grant legal recognition to Christmas. By 1890, all the states and territories had made similar acknowledgment. Christmas is the only annual religious holiday to receive official secular sanction.

## November and December
## Weekly Activity Schedule

No matter how often we tell ourselves that this year is going to be different, that we're going to stop giving so much, eating so much, and expecting so much—it just doesn't seem to happen that way.

Disappointments and expectations seem greater than at any other time of the year. Families are not really the picture-perfect photos we see portrayed in magazines and on greeting cards. Hearts are never quite as giving and forgiving as we would like them to be. Feelings get hurt and tensions run high.

There is a lot to do, and it's all being added to a schedule which may have been just barely workable before the holidays. Jobs, car pools, meals, laundry, illness, homework, etc. still exist and need attention. Use the "Week 1" form at the end of this chapter to help you get organized.

Our world doesn't stop because the calendar says it's holiday time, so be kind to yourself and ask for help. Keep those goals and expectations realistic and spend time celebrating the part of Christmas that means the most to you. If you don't have time to bake this year and you've always done it, don't do it. Find a good bakery or pay a teen to bake for you.

---

*There is a time for everything, and a season for every activity under heaven*—Ecclesiastes 3:1 (NIV).

---

## Second Week in November

It takes so little time to save time. The selection of your Christmas cards can be made in October or the first part of November. But the best way is to have purchased your cards at the 50-percent-off discounts right after the previous Christmas. Christmas cards are personal selections and should be thought through. Does the card say what you feel as a family? What message do you want to convey? With rising postal costs and increasingly busy schedules, many people have geared down on card-giving, and correspondence in general. Christmas-card-sending may be the only news we send or receive all year.

If you send cards, you will receive them. Nothing takes the stress out of a hectic day in December like sitting down with a letter or note from an old friend. It's a gift in itself. However, with every card you send, take the time to jot a few lines of what's happening. A card with just a signature is cold and impersonal. I feel that if you are going to take the time and expense to send out cards, there should be more than just a card with a signature.

Keep an updated record of the cards you send. We've provided a "Christmas Card Record" chart at the end of this chapter. As you receive cards, check to see if the return addresses are the same as what you have. Make any changes right away so you are sure to have the correct address for next year.

If you don't want to invest in cards, send postcards. The postage is less and there's room enough for a personal message.

If you have a lot of family news, consider photocopying a letter. This may be important to do the year you have moved, added a new baby, or done something truly newsworthy. Otherwise, keep your messages short.

Set up a Christmas-card station if room is available, or set up a card table and have everything collected in one spot: stamps, colored pens, address labels, address book, etc. You can address your envelopes ahead of time and write notes as you have time here or there. Don't forget to recruit help from the family and work together.

If you use printed cards, write a short note to add a personal touch, or have the children sign their names by themselves. Ten minutes of your time to write a note can mean more than a gift. Enclose a photo to friends whom you haven't seen for a year or more. I have an album of Christmas photos from friends, and we have watched children grow through these pictures.

We use and market a beautiful Christmas memory book for keeping 25 years of Christmas memories. For each year there is a spot for a holiday family photo, for the Christmas card sent that year, and for a written account of the year's events.

We think these books are so special that we make them available at all our seminars. It also makes a perfect wedding gift. If we had started one when we first married, we would be well into our second book. I'll never forget the story of a young bride, Cecila, married to Dr. Dick Patchett, an ophthalmologist. She purchased one of our Christmas Memory Books and was so excited as she showed the book to her new husband. He looked it over and then asked, "Where's the second book?" "What do you mean, second book?" bubbled Cecila. "We'll be married more than 25 years, and one won't be enough." She quickly got another book.

We take our family Christmas photo every Thanksgiving. That is one time we all seem to be together. It's fun, too, if you can co-ordinate your clothing. Be creative and do your own thing. Include the pets, teddy bears, and favorite dolls or toys.

Make up your Christmas gift list early in November. Be sure to list everyone you want to remember—from the newspaper boy to your dentist. Don't forget anyone who has been special to you and extra helpful this past year.

We've given you a chart to help organize the gift-giving di-lemma. (See "Gifts Given" chart at end of chapter.) This helps me to remember who gets what. I do a lot of food and food basket giv-ing. I need that list by my side as I put together my holiday love baskets. You can also refer back to your list to make sure you aren't repeating gifts.

We've also given you a chart for recording gifts received. (See "Gifts Received" chart at end of chapter.) With all the excitement on Christmas morning, it's hard to remember who gave you what. Keep a record of each gift as it's opened. Then, once a thank you has been written, check the appropriate blank.

It's still early November, and if you didn't buy your gift wrap after Christmas last year, now is the time to do it. Keep a good supply of scotch tape; gift tags; red, green, and white ribbon; and lots of tissue paper.

Gift tags can be made ahead of time from last year's Christmas cards—a great cut-and-paste project for children. Tags can also be made from matching wrapping paper cut into different shapes: stars, angels, teddy bears, squares, hearts, etc.

Continuing into the first week of November, you should seriously be purchasing Christmas gifts—especially those which need to be mailed out of state or out of the country. We will cover rules for mailing in another section.

## Third Week in November

Check your Christmas-card list. Update names and addresses and decide if you will send one to everyone you know or just to those people who live out of town.

People will start hunting for gift ideas for you and other members of the family (see end of chapter). Make a "wish list" for yourself. I really struggle with this, but Bob and the children have no problem making up their lists, and it's wonderful to know what they want and/or need. I am learning not to be bashful with my wishes. Remember to update sizes for the children when telling grandparents so exchanges are kept to a minimum.

Bake early and freeze food, if possible. It will make your last-minute list go a lot easier. Rolls, breads, and even some desserts freeze beautifully.

## Fourth Week in November

It's only the fourth week in November, so let's get a good jump on organization.

Find shipping boxes, wrap, and ship all out-of-state Christmas gifts, if possible, before December 1.

If you haven't already done so, send out any holiday invitations for parties, potlucks, Christmas teas, open houses, or any gatherings you are planning. By doing this early, people will make their plans around yours. (See "Hospitality Sheet" chart at end of chapter.)

Advent will begin soon, so if you plan on having an Advent wreath with candles or Advent calendars for the children, get them out now. If you plan to purchase an Advent calendar this year, look for a Christ-centered one—try your Christian bookstore. Find one that has Scriptures and/or tells the Christmas story. As each window is opened, it will give you and the family an opportunity to follow the events leading up to Christ's birth.

Check your church calendar, newspaper, or community bulletin for special Advent events.

---

*Glory to God in the highest, and on earth, peace
to men on whom his favor rests*—Luke 2:14 (NIV).

---

## First Week of December

Finish up Christmas-gift shopping and don't forget the gift wrap, batteries, film, tree-ornament hooks, or any other items you might need. Did you remember to put on your gift list a small remembrance for your postal person, receptionist, church secretary, trashman, dentist, doctor, pediatrician, or any other person who has served you well this past year?

Once you have made your major purchases, remind yourself you are finished so you won't be tempted to buy more than you intended just because you suddenly get the Christmas spirit! Leave some things such as stocking stuffers until the last minute if it makes you happy to be a part of the hustle and bustle.

Pamper yourself. Think about your holiday wardrobe. Does

anything need to be cleaned, hemmed, pressed, or altered? Do you need to add new accessories to freshen up the old basic Christmas dress? Schedule time for a mid-December hair appointment, manicure, or maybe a massage. Do whatever time and finances will allow, but do treat yourself to a rejuvenating experience, if at all possible. And try to get plenty of sleep and exercise.

---

## How to Spend Within Your Holiday Means

*By Thanksgiving at the latest, realistically estimate how much you can afford to spend. Then, make out a list of people to whom you want to give gifts, what you would like to buy for each person, along with the approximate price of the item. A quick total may show that you must scale back on the amount spent for each person or trim the number of people on your list. Take the list with you when you shop and stick to it!*

*Don't forget to budget for the "hidden costs" of Christmas. These include tree decorations, gift wrap, Christmas cards, and postage, and any entertaining you do.*

*To avoid being haunted by the ghosts of Christmas credit past, use cash or a check whenever possible. Using cash slows down your spending and forces you to weigh your purchases more carefully.*

*If you must use charge cards, clip half an index card to the back of the credit card. Each time you use it, enter the amount of your purchase on the index card and keep a running total, so that you are continually aware of how much you will have to come up with when the bills start rolling in during January.*

*Say no to holiday charge accounts that allow you to buy now and delay payment until February (unless you have an assured bonus or other cash reserve coming to cover your bill). The allure of "free money" is a trap you would be wise to avoid.*

*Ensure that you will be able to do next year's buying in cash by estimating how much your Christmas spending will be, dividing that amount into 12 monthly allotments, and then setting aside that amount each month in either a Christmas club or a money market account.*

Plan your holiday entertaining menus for Christmas Eve and/or Christmas Day. If you have room in your freezer, purchase your turkey early. If you are having a fresh turkey, goose, or ham, place your order now.

Decide what table linens you will be using and Scotchguard them; it's a great fabric protector. Spills will be easier to remove.

Keep candles in the freezer until ready for use. That way they don't have a tendency to drip or spark when lit.

Plan several baking days and put these on your calendar. Have at least one day with the children to make those special Christmas cookies and gingerbread men. That way mentally you will be prepared for the mess—dough, powdered sugar, colored frosting, coconut, and sugar all over the children. Let it be fun for them. How proud they will be when they serve a plate of their own creations!

Your days or evenings of cooking can be spent making and freezing hors d'oeuvres, casseroles, fruitcakes, plum puddings, or anything else which should have time to mellow. Not only will the food mellow, but you will also feel mellower because you've gotten a good start on a busy holiday.

Begin addressing Christmas cards if you haven't already.

Having trouble with candles standing up? Twist a rubber band around the base before inserting the candle into the holder. Or keep candles firmly in place by putting a little florist's clay in the holder.

When candles drip on your pretty tablecloths, fear not. Lay paper towels on the ironing board over and under the drips and iron the wax spots with a medium-to-hot iron. Keep moving the paper towels until the wax is absorbed into them. Presto! The wax is gone and the cloth is saved.

Put up Christmas decorations such as wreaths, garlands, candles, nativity scenes, front-door decorations, and bows. String up the outdoor lights. This is a good project for teenagers—they love climbing ladders and getting on roofs. They could make themselves available to do it for the neighborhood and make extra Christmas money or do it as a ministry to people in the church. A cup of hot cider and Christmas cookies is good payment for a hardworking, hungry teen.

---

## The Story of Santa Claus

*Many people do not know that there is a special story about who Santa Claus really was. There was a special Christian man who lived a long time ago. His name was Nicholas, and we call him St. Nicholas because saint means "someone who belongs to God." In St. Nicholas's town there were many poor children. They didn't have enough food, clothes, or toys. St. Nicholas used his money to buy food, clothes, and toys for the poor children. He didn't want them to be embarrassed by his gifts, so he gave them secretly.*

*St. Nicholas also told everyone about Jesus and how much God loved them. Many people became Christians because of what St. Nicholas said. Then some mean people who hated Jesus put St. Nicholas in jail to keep him from telling people about Jesus and helping people. St. Nicholas continued to tell people about Jesus until the mean people finally had him killed.*

*Because of how much St. Nicholas loved Jesus, and because of the many gifts he gave the poor children in his town, we still remember St. Nicholas at Christmastime. All of the gifts he gave and all of the gifts we give are to remind us of the very best gift anyone ever gave…when God the Father gave His only Son, Jesus Christ, to us for our salvation.*

—Gretchen Passantino, *Discipleship Journal*

---

Review your list again for holiday entertaining and menu planning. Keep filling the freezer with yummy baked items. What special love gifts these are for friends and neighbors—especially for the busy working woman whose time is so limited.

A fun idea is to give a favorite recipe and with it include one or two ingredients. One of my favorites is a triple-chocolate-cake recipe. Everyone loves it, and it's so easy—only three steps and five minutes. This is one I couldn't live without for any last-minute special dessert.

I give the recipe and include a package of chocolate chips, a box of chocolate pudding, and the box of chocolate cake mix.

### ✇ Emilie's Triple Chocolate Fudge Cake

*Amount:* 10 to 12 servings

Prepare 1 3¾-ounce package of chocolate pudding mix (cooked type) as directed on package. Blend chocolate cake mix (dry mix) into hot pudding. Pour ingredients into prepared oblong pan, 13" x 9½" x 2".

Sprinkle with ½ cup semisweet chocolate pieces and ½ cup chopped nuts. Bake 30 to 35 minutes at 350°. Serve warm with whipped cream or ice cream—also delicious plain.

Following are great recipes for Christmas Spiced Tea and Holiday Wassail. Make a double batch and divide it into small, attractive jars. Put on a holiday label with instructions and tie a red ribbon around each jar. Your gift recipient will love it and enjoy the special thought for the holiday season.

### ✇ Christmas Spiced Tea

*Amount:* makes 1½ quarts

    1 cup instant tea (dry) (can use decaffeinated)
    2 cups dry lemonade mix (orange flavor)
    3 cups sugar (may use 1½ cups sugar substitute and
        1½ cups sugar)
    ½ cup red hots (candy)
    1 teaspoon cinnamon
    ½ teaspoon powdered cloves
    ½ package dry lemonade mix (8 ounces)

To one cup of hot water, add one heaping tablespoon of mix.

Gifts don't have to be expensive. The effort and love that you put into your homemade gifts will be especially appreciated.

Make a batch of bran muffins. You can give the recipe, a muffin tin, and six muffins in the tin. Wrap the tin with clear cellophane wrap, tie a bell and pretty bow on top, and share your love of muffins with your family and friends.

---

*The word became flesh and made his dwelling among us. We have seen his glory, the glory of the One and Only, who came from the Father, full of grace and truth*—John 1:14 (NIV).

---

When I have a holiday party, open house, or tea, I serve my Holiday Wassail. It has received lots of compliments and makes the house smell festive and wonderful.

## ☙ *Holiday Wassail Recipe*

    1 gallon apple cider
    1 large can pineapple juice (unsweetened)
    $^3/_4$ cup strong tea (herb tea optional)

*In a cheesecloth sack put:*
    1 tablespoon whole cloves
    1 tablespoon whole allspice
    2 sticks cinnamon

This is great cooked in a Crockpot. Let it simmer slowly for four to six hours. You can add water if it evaporates too much. Your house will smell wonderful, and friends and family will love it!

## Second Week of December

Finish wrapping your Christmas presents and update your gift list. This will lessen last-minute gift-wrapping. Do you have a good hiding place for the children's gifts? If not, consider asking a neighbor to swap hiding places with you.

If you made any catalog purchases, check your orders. Has everything arrived? If not, call the customer service department and inquire. Remember your quiet and gentle spirit! The customer service representatives may be frazzled and not as organized as you are. Shop for necessary gift substitutes or have Plan B ready if the order doesn't arrive in time.

The time frame for decorating is a personal or family decision. We like to have our decorations up for the whole month, so we begin early. Our tree goes up by the second week in December. It may be fun to get a few things out each day for a week or so, culminating your efforts with the trimming of the tree. This makes it easier for the busy woman and fun for the kids, too.

---

### The Candy Cane

*I searched through the town, looking at all the "trappings" of the season, the santas and the reindeer, the stockings and the elves, hoping to find the real meaning of Christmas. Then, there it was...the candy cane. The legend is that it was invented by a Christian in England in the seventeenth century. At that time, the government would not let people celebrate Christmas. So, a candy maker made candy shaped like a shepherd's crook to be a secret symbol of Jesus. The white stripe represented the purity of Jesus and the red stripe represented His life that He gave for each of us. The candy was a double gift: a sweet treat and a symbol of Christmas.*

My friend, Ginny Pasqualucci, keeps her decorations up well into January because she loves Christmas so much. Recently, she went to the Holy Land for Christmas. They had us over for dinner on January 29 for a full Christmas evening, complete with Bing Crosby singing "White Christmas," with all the decorations still up and gifts under their two trees. It was wonderful. So do whatever you prefer—it's kosher.

Remember those replacement bulbs for your light strings? Do you have enough for tree-trimming day, plus ornament hangers for the ornaments?

Make tree-trimming a special time of fun. Play Christmas tapes and light a few candles if it is during the evening. Make an easy meal, or you could have a cookie-and-hot-spiced-tea platter ready for "halftime." This is a good time to pull a casserole from the freezer for dinner.

If you are planning a Christmas Eve potluck or buffet, review your menu. This can become a tradition. One week before, each family member can plan a dish to serve. Prepare the dish a day or two ahead. After Christmas Eve services, spread out the buffet near the tree on snack tables. You can have a sing-along, read the Bible, and serve communion.

The Christmas breakfast brunch menu, if you're serving one, should be checked. Make sure you have all the ingredients you need in your pantry.

Plan your table settings and centerpiece.

---

*Thank you, God, for quiet places far from life's crowded ways, where our hearts find true contentment and our souls fill up with praise*—Author unknown.

# Third Week of December

The countdown continues. Double-check your shopping lists, supplies, menus, etc. You may have parties to attend yourself. Save the invitations until you have written your thank-you notes. Take a baked goodie, some Christmas Spiced Tea, or a handmade ornament as a hostess gift.

If your tree didn't go up last week, this may be the week to put it up. You may want to invite friends to help make it a festive event. String fresh popcorn or cranberries (this takes patience).

Check your holiday calendar for this week and next, including special church services that you will want to attend. Are you beginning to feel overwhelmed—hustled, hurried, and hassled? If so, prioritize events and extend regrets to those you really don't have to attend. You need time for yourself if you are going to enjoy the next two weeks. It's okay to say no.

Make a list of holiday telephone calls you want to make to family and friends and begin making them now. The circuits will be very busy on Christmas Eve and Christmas Day, and you don't want to spend all your time dialing the phone.

---

*But the angel said to them, "Do not be afraid. I bring you good news of great joy that will be for all the people. Today in the town of David a Savior has been born to you; he is Christ the Lord"*—Luke 2:10-11 (NIV).

---

Many families have a birthday cake for Jesus. This can be made ahead and frozen. One mom shared an idea with her family of having a birthday cake for Jesus complete with candles. They decided to do it after the presents were opened on Christmas morning. Another family has a very simple party at the end of Christmas Day—with packages all opened, paper everywhere, and dirty dishes.

They take ten minutes and sing "Happy Birthday, Jesus," blow out the candles on a cake, and have a quiet family communion. The eating of the cake is not what is important. That can be done another day if tummies are too full. The purpose is to focus on the real meaning of Christmas.

## Christmas Week

There's not much left to do—we have our plan, and the plan is working.

Go over the menus and supplies one more time. Any last-minute purchases necessary? Shop for groceries.

Try to keep normal routines, if possible, because small children sense the excitement and can be overwhelmed. Schedule reading times with them. Our grandchildren love the Christmas story all year long—they love to hear it over and over. Talk about what the true meaning of Christmas is—how we give gifts just as the wise men brought gifts to the Christ child.

Place the wrapped gifts under the tree, if you haven't already done so. If you open most of the gifts on Christmas Day, consider letting each child open one early. It may be the most appreciated gift.

Keep the list of gifts received up-to-date as each present is opened. This makes writing thank-you notes much easier.

Check your stocking-stuffer items and have them ready to fill on Christmas Eve—late. If Santa comes to your house, leave a snack for him—and don't forget a carrot for Rudolph!

Set your Christmas Eve and/or Christmas Day tables a few days ahead. Put out those serving dishes labeled with the 3" x 5" cards.

Relax and enjoy yourself and your family. Have a very Merry Christmas. You've worked hard and planned well. You deserve a blessed Christmas.

# Parcel Post Shopping Hints

This is the time of year when post office lobbies draw crowds. The U.S. Postal Service's first rule at this time of year is "the earlier the better." Here are additional tips for ensuring that your mail arrives in time for the holidays.

1. *Containers*—The postal service says fiberboard boxes, such as those available at grocery stores and other retailers, are ideal. Popular-sized boxes and mailing envelopes or bags are available at stationers and post office branches.

2. *Packing*—Cushion box contents with crumpled newspaper. Place the paper around all sides, corners, top, and bottom so the contents won't move, even if you shake the box. Foam shells, "popcorn," and padding are sold for cushioning and may be worth the investment if the items you're planning to send are particularly fragile. Mark the package in three places if the contents are fragile: above the address, below the postage, and on the reverse side.

   Padded mailing envelopes or bags are ideal for small items, including books. Avoid using twine, cord, or string. No wrapping paper is allowed on the outside of packages. With boxes, brown paper is not necessary. Put a slip of paper with the name and address of the recipient inside the box, as well as on the outside.

3. *Sealing*—Close the carton with one of the three recommended types of tape: pressure-sensitive, nylon-reinforced paper, or glass-reinforced pressure sensitive. No scotch tape, please!

4. *Addressing*—Use smudge-proof ink. Put the recipient's name and address in the lower right portion of the package. Cover the label with clear tape to waterproof. Put your return address in the upper left corner of only one side of the package. Remove all other labels from the box. Use correct zip codes—a wrong zip code can delay delivery.

5. *Christmas cards*—Holiday cards must be in standard-size en-velopes at least 3½" high and 5" long. If the card is extra large, you will have to pay extra postage. If in doubt, have the enve-lope measured by a postal clerk.

Mail not only early in the month, but also early in the day. If you are mailing across the continent, the U.S. Postal Service ad-vises allowing eight to ten days for packages and cards.

When mailing a gift-wrapped present, stuff the package into a dry cleaning plastic bag with crumpled newspapers outside the bag as buffers. That way the newsprint won't rub off on the wrapping paper. Protect the bow from being crushed by covering it with a plastic berry basket—the type strawberries come in.

## Surviving the Stress of Shopping

Busy women today don't even want to think about Christmas until after Thanksgiving. We simply haven't had the time to get into stores to shop. We have had meetings to attend and deadlines to meet. The teacher whose energies went into the classroom and who postponed shopping until school was out is now faced with a dilemma. Even many retailers who have been busy selling to others haven't had time themselves to buy gifts. We all share a common expression: "Help!" However, there is hope. Organization is the key to the task. We all have limited time. Every minute we spend in the stores must have a purpose. Before we begin, we must plan our shopping strategy.

*She will give birth to a son, and you are to give him the name Jesus, because he will save his people from their sins*—Matthew 1:21 (NIV).

1. In your mind review all the stores in a center or mall. Perhaps a better idea is to write them down: bookstore, china shop, hardware store, jewelry store, clothing shop, etc. Hopefully you can accomplish the majority of your shopping in one trip.

2. Make a list based on the shops within a particular mall. Work your way around mentally, jotting down specific people.

3. Take advantage of wrapping services and/or gift boxes, ribbon, and tissue. Have as many gifts as you can ready to place under the tree when you arrive home.

4. Do two things at once. If, for example, you purchase clothing for three people which includes gift-wrapping, allow the clerks to finish the packages while you visit other shops. Circle back at the end of the day and collect your packages.

5. Decide before you go out if this year you are purchasing "one big gift" or lots of little things. Each year I do things a bit differently.

6. Give something an unusual touch. For example, if you are giving a cookbook, wrap it in a tea towel or add an apron or muffin tin. If it's a piece of jewelry, include a nightshirt. Compress your gift into a can or a jar.

---

### Christmas Prayer

*May the spirit of giving*
*Go on through the year,*
*Bringing love, laughter,*
*Hope, and good cheer.*
*Gifts wrapped with charity,*
*Joy, peace, and grace,*
*Ribboned with happiness,*
*A tender embrace.*

—Norma Woodbridge

7. Think in categories: How many golfers, skiers, and tennis players are on your list? If buying for one, buy for three. What about duplicate gifts? Can you give all your neighbors a soup mix or the gourmet cheese or spiced-mustard jar? Absolutely! Many times one stop will take care of five or six gifts.

8. You can also use the phone to your advantage. Call your florist to make up a unique silk arrangement in a basket of soaps and hand cream, etc. The shop will often wrap and deliver the baskets for you. And anyone would love to receive a pretty holiday arrangement with a candle to use as a Christmas table centerpiece.

9. For the hard-to-please and those people who have everything, a gift certificate for a restaurant, ice cream shop, or fast-food restaurant (children love that) are always a hit.

10. Take a few breaks during your shopping to review your list and collect your thoughts. Plan a coffee, tea, or lunch break. You will also need to make periodic trips to lock the packages in your car.

11. Don't leave the shopping area until you are sure you have accomplished all you wanted to do in that spot. Retracing your steps or making second trips isn't practical.

12. Ask a teenager or a friend who loves to shop to pick something up for you.

13. Remember to keep it simple. The love you put into each gift will be what lasts. This season is the time for warmth, fellowship, shared experiences, and hospitality.

14. Hire your teenagers to help out by running errands, wrapping gifts, tying bows, preparing food, sending out party invitations, etc. This is a great teaching time for them.

15. Plan a family conference time when you all can decide what items rate as top priorities. Reconfirm what needs to be done

and what's not so meaningful this year. If the front-door wreath or a nativity scene on the mantel are essential, put these on the list of "to dos." If, on the other hand, no one cares about making gingerbread cookies, scratch them off the list.

16. As a group, decide how much is to be spent on presents. There is no point in starting the new year with huge bills and a lot of guilt.

17. Keep your sense of humor and perspective. Make it fun. The whole point is to see the season in terms of memories and lasting values. What is the heart of the celebration? If togetherness and a spirit of giving are concepts you want to teach, preserve, and nurture, build on these for this month of Christmas.

18. Spend time together making cookies, framing photographs to give to grandparents, assembling baskets of goodies for the neighbors, directing and filming your own Christmas video, or just gathering around the fireplace for hot cider and good talk. These are the times you will treasure long after the gift wrap and food scraps have gone into the trash.

---

*Suddenly a great company of the heavenly host appeared with the angel, praising God and saying, "Glory to God in the highest, and on earth peace to men on whom his favor rests"*—Luke 2:13-14.

## How to Keep Holidays Stressless

Here are a few hints and tips to keep your holidays more stress-free.

1. Ask your family members to share their favorite holiday memory. You may be surprised how few meals and toys they mention.

We did this at our church Christmas party one year and, to my surprise, very few people could recall special holiday memories. If this is the case, create some memories. Make your time count. A memory lasts forever, but toys get broken.

2. Settle family matters before holiday time. Families are often separated by divorce or geographic distance, and disputes can arise. Try to make all the arrangements well ahead of time. If you have out-of-town guests, decide where they will stay and let them know before they arrive if they will need a hotel room. Share your time equally and fairly with each set of grandparents, or take turns from year to year. Avoid overcommitment—it can make for situations where people are overtired and overreact.

3. Don't gain weight. Feeling fat in party clothes can really add to your stress and tension. Overeating can make you feel absolutely awful. Try to schedule the same exercise you normally do. If you are not exercising now, make it a goal for the new year.

   There will be a great deal of extra goodies around, so be selective about what you eat. Stick to the things that are worth it—like your favorites that you see only at holiday time.

   Only go past the part of the food table where the fruit or veggie platter is. If you decide now not to overdo it, you won't have to make a New Year's resolution later to lose weight.

4. Remember what really matters. As Christians, Christmas is the time for celebrating the birth of Christ, and everything else comes after that special celebration. The hassles will take care of themselves.

5. Watch your finances carefully. Talk about tension and depression! Overspending will do it, especially if you've overcharged and have those bills to look forward to later. Ask the Lord to help you in this area so you won't get caught up in the spirit of things and buy much more than you budgeted for.

   Remember that a handmade gift or baked item can be more valuable than an expensive present. Special phone calls or a coupon for an "after-Christmas lunch treat" can mean as much to friends as an expensive gift they may or may not use or like. Set your budget and stick to it. Many people have a special Christmas fund set aside. That makes it easy and, when that's gone, it's gone. Otherwise, spread your purchases over a period of time and charge only the amount you intend to spend. That's why we suggest you begin your gift shopping early in November so it doesn't all come at once.

6. It's okay to say no. You would like to do it all, be everywhere, and see everything. But for today's busy woman, it just can't be. Don't be afraid to say, "No, we need this time together as a family," or "No, I can't bake the extra cookies, but I'd be happy to buy some." Don't feel guilty about those things you simply cannot do.

7. Plan some time for yourself. You can read a book, listen to a music tape, take a bubble bath by candlelight, get a good haircut, have your nails polished, or maybe even buy yourself a new nightgown, blouse, or holiday sweater. By taking care of yourself, that last-minute hassle about your appearance won't happen.

8. Christmas will come regardless if you have done everything on your lists or not. Do those things which really matter and let the others fall where they may.

Family, friends, and above all, the true meaning of Christmas, are what count. Remember: 85 percent of our stress is caused by disorganization.

---

*So they [the shepherds] hurried off and found Mary and Joseph, and the baby, who was lying in the manger—Luke 2:16.*

# Decorating and Entertaining Ideas

The most important entertaining you will do this year, and especially during the Christmas season, will be for your own family. In our home it's a special time for all of us. I bring out what china, crystal, and silver I have for these family times. The children have learned to handle the dishes gently, and it makes for treasured learning times. Even if you don't have these kinds of items, bring out your best—whatever it is: paper, plastic, metal, china, or crystal. Don't let the lack of things prevent you from decorating and entertaining.

1. *Sheets for tablecloths*—I have fun mixing and matching my table settings. Here are a few ideas I use to make my tables creative and different. Regardless of what the holiday may be, I use sheets for making tablecloths and napkins. I'll take the saucer from my set of eight dishes to the store to look for sheets that might match or coordinate. Many times I'll find a sheet on sale that will work perfectly. I keep my eyes open all year for white sales, and I've found some great bargains.

   To make one tablecloth and 12 napkins for a standard-size table, use a king-size flat sheet. If you don't want so many napkins, or if you have a small table, you can use a full- or queen-size sheet. A twin sheet will do if you don't want matching napkins. (You can make six napkins out of one yard of coordinating fabric. Cut each napkin 15" square.) It is quite alright to leave the sheet's border on the tablecloth, if you wish. People don't usually go around to see if you have a border on the other side.

   Measure the length and width of your table and add six inches to hang over each side. Then add one inch for a turn-under hem. Cut your tablecloth out first. Then make your napkins out of the remainder. A nice size for napkins is 18" square, but you may want a smaller napkin.

   If you are making a round tablecloth, fold the sheet in half and cut a string the length of the radius of your table plus the six-inch drop and one-inch hem. Mark your half-circle cutting line with pins or chalk. Cut your napkins out right next to each other. It's always nice to finish the napkins with lace or eyelet embroidery.

I continue to look for Christmas sheets, but so far haven't found any with poinsettias, holly, or red-and-green prints or stripes. Many times I have to settle for holiday fabric such as taffeta, felt, or even lace panel curtains. I bought a lace panel curtain at K-Mart for $5.99 one year and made a tablecloth. I also made six napkins and one lace runner from it.

A green or red felt fabric tablecloth is great for Christmas. You can buy felt by the yard. It doesn't have to be hemmed, and it's nice and wide so no sewing is needed. Also, today's new felt is completely washable. It looks beautiful as is, or you can add a plaid runner, taffeta overcloth, or even holiday place mats. Napkin rings can be made with taffeta ribbon by tying a bow around the napkin.

2. *Napkin rings*—Cover empty toilet paper rolls with lace and cut the rolls 2" to 3" in width for simple but nice napkin rings.

Paint wooden clothespins red, green, or white to clip on your napkins. Names can be personalized with a paint pen from the craft store.

Using quilted fabric, cut a boot, star, or angel, leaving an opening at the top for a napkin. The fabric can be sewn or glue-gunned together.

Cookie cutters (plastic or metal) make great napkin rings. You can find them in gourmet stores, kitchen sections of department stores, and catalogs. They come in all shapes.

Napkin rings can be made out of many different materials. One year we were having 26 people for our family Christmas dinner. I was using an old standby poinsettia fabric tablecloth I had used previously, but I wanted to jazz it up a bit. I found some wooden napkin rings—cheap! I bought some red silk poinsettia flowers (small version), cut off the long stem, and glue-gunned the flower to the plain wooden rings. It was sensational with my green napkins, but the best part was I had 26 matching napkin rings for less than 25 cents each. I've used them for the past four years. They store well and keep their shape as long as I put them in my numbered storage boxes.

If you want to go fancy, start collecting china napkin rings. Buy two to four each year until you have enough for your table, or let your family know you're collecting them. It's a great gift idea.

Here's an idea for a Christ-centered napkin ring. Take your paper towel tube and cut it in two-inch widths. Then cut each ring so it opens. Write a Scripture inside and, with your glue gun or regular glue, cover the outside with ribbon, leaving tails long enough on each side of the opening to tie a bow. Slide your napkin through the ring. When your family members or guests untie the bow, there in front of their eyes will be God's Word. If you have each person read his or her verse, it can become the prayer of blessing.

3. *China collection*—Thirty-nine years ago when Bob and I were married, I shared with my family that I would like to collect china cups and saucers. Since that time, I have received over 37 gifts of beautiful cups and saucers, all different. I use them often, letting our guests pick out a favorite they would like to use that evening. I also have several different dinner plates that don't match, and it's so much fun to set a table with all the different plates and cups. They have become conversation pieces. I have also found some great buys on china plates at garage and estate sales. It's a fun hobby, and I use the plates and cups often.

I found a terrific buy at a bargain store. They were selling solid-red ceramic plates at 88 cents each. I use these red plates for Christmas with the green felt tablecloth and the red poinsettia napkin rings. The red plates come out again for Valentine's Day with pink and white napkins, and again on the Fourth of July for our red, white, and blue patio party. It's been a great investment.

4. *Centerpieces*—For a centerpiece, it's attractive to arrange several different-size candles at different heights (maybe six to ten candles). When lit, they make a beautiful arrangement, and yet it is so simple.

Tie a plaid Christmas bow around the base of your candles or around the candle holder itself. You can change the ribbons and bows for all seasons and holidays.

A pretty centerpiece is a wreath set on a glass plate on the table with candles in the center. Use your creativity with pinecones, poinsettias, flowers, ribbon, moss, ivy, and holly.

Make Christmas trees, gingerbread men, or small stuffed teddy bears in Christmas fabrics. Tie a bow around the neck of each bear. These can be placed against each person's water glass as a gift to remember the evening in your home.

Teddy bears are universal and versatile. They can be used for hugging, loving, and sharing. Write a Scripture verse on a piece of paper and roll it up and insert it through the ribbon around teddy's neck. Not only do your guests take home a teddy bear, but they also take home God's Word.

## Two Holiday Menus

---

*Emilie's Orange Chicken*

*Brown Rice or Almond Brown Rice*

*Holiday Tomatoes & Steamed Broccoli*

*Tossed Salad with Emilie's Olive Oil Dressing*

*Carrot Bran Muffins*

*No-Bake Honey Cheesecake*

---

> Baked Parmesan Chicken
> Brown or Wild Rice Pilaf
> Christmas Red & Green Beans
> Tossed Salad with Emilie's Olive Oil Dressing
> Lemon Ginger Muffins
> Ambrosia

## ∽ Emilie's Orange Chicken

*Amount:* 4 to 6 servings

1. In a saucepan combine and heat while stirring until butter and jelly are melted and sauce is smooth:

   1 cup orange juice
   ½ cup (1 stick) butter
   ½ cup red currant jelly
   ¼ cup Worcestershire sauce
   2 large cloves garlic, crushed
   1 tablespoon Dijon mustard
   1 teaspoon powdered ginger
   3 dashes Tabasco sauce

2. Cool sauce.

3. Place in baking pan:

   1 whole chicken, skinned and quartered, or
       8 skinless chicken breast pieces

4. Pour sauce over all; marinate in refrigerator for 2 to 3 hours.

5. Preheat oven to 350°.

6. Cover chicken and bake for 1 hour. Uncover, increase temperature to 400° and continue to bake, basting frequently until chicken is an even dark brown.

## ∞ Baked Parmesan Chicken

*Amount:* 6 servings

1. Melt in baking pan at about 250°:

　½ cup (1 stick) butter

2. Meanwhile, mix in blender until small bread crumbs are formed; pour into shallow bowl:

　1 slice whole wheat bread (or as needed to make 1 cup)
　2 sprigs parsley (or about ¼ cup minced)
　½ cup parmesan cheese
　⅛ teaspoon salt
　⅛ teaspoon garlic powder

3. Skin and remove visible fat from chicken:

　2 pounds boneless chicken breast pieces

4. Coat pieces of chicken in melted butter in pan, then coat with crumb mixture; lay single layer in remaining butter in pan.

5. Garnish with paprika and bake uncovered at 350° until tender (about 1 hour); baste 2 or 3 times during baking. Cover with foil if chicken begins to brown too much before it's done.

*Reduced Fat Version* (reduces the calories of fat by 29%!):

1. Reduce parmesan cheese to 3 tablespoons.

2. Omit the butter. Dip chicken pieces before coating with crumbs in nonfat milk (amount as needed).

3. Spray baking pan with no-stick cooking spray (Olive Oil Pam Spray preferred).

## ∞ Brown Rice

Chewy, flavorful, and so easy to prepare! For company, add a dollop of sour cream to dress up each serving of Brown Rice or Almond Brown Rice.

*Amount:* 3 cups (4 to 6 servings)

1. Place together in a saucepan that has a tight-fitting lid, bring to a boil, and boil uncovered for 5 minutes:

   2 to 2½ cups water
   1 cup long-grain brown rice (see note below)
   up to 1 teaspoon salt (optional)

2. Turn heat very low, cover pan with a tight-fitting lid, and simmer for 50 to 65 minutes. Do not lift lid during cooking. If you do, you will get sticky rice. To test for doneness, insert a spoon straight down through the rice to the bottom of the pot and press a bit of rice to one side. If no unabsorbed water remains, taste the rice to see if it is tender. If not done, cover and cook another 10 minutes or until done.

*Note:* Long-grain brown rice is less chewy and sticky than medium- or short-grain brown rice, and is closer to the texture of white rice. Most people prefer this texture.

## ∞ Almond Brown Rice

A simple, yet delightful, variation on plain brown rice. Use the whole wheat kernel or berry, not ground or milled wheat.

*Amount:* 4 cups (6 to 8 servings)

1. Follow the recipe for Brown Rice with these changes:

   use 2½ cups water
   add ¼ cup whole wheat kernels (from health-food store) or wild rice
   add ¼ cup almonds (chopped, slivered, or sliced)

2. For a little gourmet flare of added flavor, sauté almonds in 1 tablespoon butter and add to the cooked rice. For color, sauté a chopped green onion with the almonds during the last minute, or garnish cooked rice with fresh chopped parsley.

---

*Do not forget to entertain strangers, for by so doing some people have entertained angels without knowing it*—Hebrews 13:2 (NIV).

## ∞ Wild Rice Pilaf

*Amount:* about 4 cups (6 to 8 servings)

1. Sauté for 20 minutes over moderately low heat in skillet, stirring often:

    ¼ cup melted butter
    1 cup uncooked wild rice
    ½ cup chopped or slivered almonds
    6 to 8 small fresh mushrooms, sliced (or 4-ounce can, drained)—add during last 5 minutes of sautéing

2. While rice is sautéing, bring to a boil in saucepan:

    3 cups chicken broth (add ½ teaspoon salt if broth is unsalted)

3. Place rice in casserole dish and pour the hot broth over rice. Add water chestnuts, cover, and bake 1½ hours at 350°.

    8-ounce can sliced water chestnuts, drained and rinsed (optional)

4. To serve, top rice with:

¼ cup chopped fresh parsley or 1 to 2 chopped green onions (lightly sautéed in water for 2 minutes).

## ∞ Brown Rice Pilaf

*Amount:* 4½ cups (6 servings)

1. Optional: Brown the rice, wheat, almonds (see amounts in step 2), stirring frequently over medium heat:

    2 tablespoons butter, melted
    2 tablespoons light olive or canola oil (health-food store)

2. Place in saucepan, bring to boil, and boil uncovered for 5 minutes:

    1¼ cups long-grain brown rice
    ¼ cup whole wheat kernels (health-food store) or wild rice, or ¼ cup more brown rice
    ¼ cup slivered or chopped almonds
    3 cups water or chicken broth
    4 teaspoons Sue's "Kitchen Magic" seasoning (use chicken broth, not water, if this seasoning is not available)
    2 teaspoons Worcestershire sauce or soy sauce

3. Cover with tight fitting lid, reduce heat to very low, and simmer 50 to 60 minutes or until all the water is absorbed and rice is tender. Do not remove lid or stir during cooking as this tends to produce sticky rice.

4. While rice cooks, lightly sauté 2 chopped green onions for a minute or two in 1 or 2 tablespoons water.

5. Fold green onions into rice just before serving. Fresh chopped parsley or freeze-dried or fresh chives can be used in place of green onions.

## ∞ Holiday Tomatoes

These are so easy to make that you don't need an exact recipe.

*Amount:* Prepare 1 to 2 halves per serving (depending on size of tomatoes)

1. Cut tomatoes in half.

2. Place in blender and crumble until fine:

   1 soft whole-wheat bread slice, broken (or amount desired)
   a sprig of fresh parsley (to make about a tablespoon
     when minced)

3. Pour into mixing bowl and blend in:

   parmesan cheese (amount desired)
   about ½ teaspoon sweet basil leaves

4. Spread about 1 tablespoon of the crumb mixture over top of each tomato half and drizzle each with:

   1 teaspoon butter

5. Set in baking pan and bake at 350° for 12 to 15 minutes.

## ∞ Broccoli

Cook it right and you will have the brightest green vegetable imaginable! The secret is to not cook it as long as most cookbooks recommend.

*Amount:* 6 servings

1. Clean and trim off tough outer skin of stalk, leaving as much of stalk end as desired:

   2 pounds broccoli

2. Place vegetable steamer basket over boiling water, add broccoli, cover, and steam for 10 minutes.

3. Serve with:

   juice of ½ lemon

*Alternative cooking method:*

1. Bring to a boil enough water to cover the broccoli.

2. Add broccoli, return to boil quickly over high heat, cover, and boil 40 to 60 seconds. That's all!

3. Drain immediately.

## ∞ Christmas Red & Green Beans

Easy! Easy! Easy!

*Amount:* 8 to 10 servings

1. Sauté onion and pepper in oil until soft:

   1 to 2 tablespoons olive oil
   1 onion, chopped
   1 green pepper, chopped

2. Drain and combine in casserole dish with:

   2 1-pound cans green beans, drained or two 10-ounce packages frozen cut green beans
   2 1-pound cans baby tomatoes

3. Optional—Brown, drain thoroughly, and add:

   6 slices bacon, broken in pieces

4. Cover and bake at 350° for 30 minutes.

## ∞ Emilie's Olive Oil Dressing

Emilie's best dressing recipe. Always a winner!

*Amount:* 1¾ cups

1. Mash together with tip of knife and put into a pint jar:

   3 cloves garlic, pressed
   1 teaspoon salt
   scant ½ teaspoon pepper

2. Add and shake well:

> 1 cup olive oil
> ½ cup wine vinegar
> juice of 1 lemon (about ¼ cup)

3. Chill thoroughly before serving.

## ∞ *Carrot Bran Muffins*

*Amount:* 12 large muffins

1. Spray muffin pan with no-stick cooking spray (Olive Oil Pam Spray preferred)

2. To soften raisins, cover with warm water and let stand 5 to 10 minutes:

> ½ cup raisins

3. Blend together and let stand for 5 minutes to soften bran:

> ½ cup boiling-hot water
> 1½ cups unprocessed wheat bran (this is not bran cereal, but plain bran without sugar, sodium, or any other ingredient added—available at supermarkets and health-food stores)

4. Blend together thoroughly with wire whisk:

> ¼ cup oil, optional
> ½ cup honey or crystalline fructose (health-food store)
> 1 or 2 eggs, or 2 or 3 egg whites

5. Mix in:

> 1 cup grated fresh carrots, or unpeeled grated zucchini
> 1 cup buttermilk
> bran mixture

6. Blend dry ingredients together in a separate bowl:

> 1½ cups whole-wheat pastry flour (health-food store)

1½ teaspoons baking soda
1 teaspoon salt
1 teaspoon cinnamon

7. Blend dry ingredients into liquid ingredients just until mixed, but do not overmix.

8. Gently fold in:

raisins, drained
½ cup chopped walnuts

9. Fill muffin cups evenly, each almost full, and bake at 350° for 20 to 25 minutes. Allow to cool 2 or more minutes until muffins can easily be removed from pan.

## ∞ *Lemon Ginger Muffins*

*Amount:* 10 large or 12 medium muffins

1. Spray muffin pan with no-stick cooking spray (Olive Oil Pam Spray preferred)

2. Prepare and set aside:

2 tablespoons fresh grated lemon peel
2 tablespoons finely chopped fresh ginger

3. Blend together and let stand (mixture will foam up):

1 cup plain yogurt or buttermilk
1 teaspoon baking soda

4. Blend well in a separate bowl:

¼ cup soft butter or oil, optional
½ cup honey or crystalline fructose (health-food store)

5. Add to honey mixture, blending thoroughly:

2 large eggs, or 4 egg whites
grated lemon and chopped ginger

6. Mix into honey-egg mixture alternately:

   yogurt or buttermilk mixture
   2 cups whole-wheat pastry flour (health-food store)—mix
      in ²/₃ cup at a time

7. Fill muffin cups almost full. If making 10 large muffins, fill the two center muffin cups halfway with water.

8. Bake at 375° for 18 to 20 minutes.

9. While muffins bake, blend together:

   ¼ cup fresh-squeezed lemon juice
   1 tablespoon honey or crystalline fructose (health-food store)

10. Cool muffins for 5 minutes. Dip top and bottom of each muffin in lemon juice mixture.

## ∞ Ambrosia

So simple to make, yet so sweetly delicious!

*Amount:* 6 servings

1. Toast about 8 minutes at 325° in shallow pan until lightly-browned:

   ½ cup medium shred coconut, unsweetened (health-food store)

2. Meanwhile, combine in mixing bowl:

   3 medium oranges or 2 mangoes, peeled and cut in chunks
   3 cups pineapple chunks, unsweetened (fresh, or
      canned that have been drained)
   6 tablespoons raisins
   1 tablespoon crystalline fructose (health-food store) or
      1 to 2 tablespoons sugar

3. Fold in toasted coconut and thoroughly chill in refrigerator to blend flavors before serving.

## ∞ No-Bake Honey Cheesecake

*Amount:* 6 to 9 servings

1. Stir gelatin into water and let stand 5 minutes to soften:

    ¼ cup cold water (room temperature is okay)
    1 package (2 teaspoons) unflavored gelatin

2. Meanwhile, mix together in blender:

    1 egg
    ⅓ cup mild-flavored honey (a lighter color usually
        indicates milder flavor)
    1 teaspoon vanilla extract

3. Gradually add, blending until no lumps remain:

    8 ounces cream cheese, softened

4. Blend in until smooth:

    ½ cup lowfat or nonfat plain yogurt
    ½ cup sour cream or light sour cream

5. Dissolve softened gelatin by bringing just to a boil over medium heat, stirring constantly, or on full power in microwave 40 to 60 seconds.

6. Thoroughly mix dissolved gelatin into remaining ingredients in the blender; pour mixture into an 8" or 9" square pan; chill until set.

7. For graham cracker topping, blend together:

    ¼ cup graham cracker crumbs
    1 tablespoon crystalline fructose (health-food store) or
        2 tablespoons sugar
    1 tablespoon melted butter

8. Sprinkle crumb topping over cheesecake anytime during chilling process or just before serving.[1]

---

*If you want to serve a traditional turkey for your main Christmas entrée, go back to the Thanksgiving chapter to find recipes and tips.*

---

## Ideas for Holiday Leftovers

My very favorite part of a big Christmas dinner is the leftovers. I will cook a turkey just for that purpose. There is something about the taste of cold turkey snitched in the kitchen on Christmas night or later in the week that is better than any feast ever served in a four-star restaurant. In fact, some of the best meals I've served have been the result of holiday leftovers. Here are some special tips for using leftovers:

1. Freshen rolls by sprinkling with water and heating in the oven, adding butter and garlic powder, if desired.

2. Make TV dinners by placing leftovers in an aluminum pan, covering with foil, and labeling before sticking in the freezer. Perfect for busy days and late suppers.

3. Leftover food should be stored within two hours, which includes serving time. Keep hot foods hot (above 165°) and cold foods cold (below 40°).

4. Freeze leftover gravy in ice-cube trays; pop out cubes and store in plastic bags. Do the same with fruit juices.

5. Freeze leftover water chestnuts tightly covered in their liquid.

6. Bits of jelly and jam can be melted in a small pan over low heat to make a good sauce for waffles, puddings, or ice cream. They also make a nice glaze.

7. Avoid storing different cakes, cookies, or breads in the same container. The flavors mix, and the baked goods don't keep as well.

8. To refresh cookies that are too soft, heat in a 300° oven just before serving. If cookies are too hard, place them in an airtight container and add a piece of apple or bread. It will take a day or two to soften them.

9. Cooked meats and vegetables should be reheated and added late in the process of assembling a casserole or cooking a soup or stew. This helps retain flavor, texture, and nutritional value.

10. See the Thanksgiving chapter to find additional tips and recipes for leftovers.

## Holiday Storage

It's over—now what?

Storage can be a very easy process and will relieve next year's stress when done properly.

Here's what you will need:

+ A good supply of white storage boxes 16" long by 12" wide by 10" deep with a lid (check your local stationery store for supplies)

+ 1 wide black felt-tip pen

+ 3" x 5" card file box

+ 3" x 5" cards

Instead of writing all over the storage box with a description of the contents, simply number your boxes #25A, #25B, #25C, etc. (25 for December 25). Then make out corresponding 3" x 5" cards numbered #25A, #25B, #25C, etc. On the left corner of each card, write the area where the box is stored. (Examples: garage, attic, cellar, closet in spare room, guest bedroom.) List on the cards exactly what you are storing in each numbered box. These cards can be stored in a 3" x 5" file box. When you need an item, just look it up in your file box and go to the storage area where the box is. It's easy, quick, and neat. If you have a computer, this information can be stored in your computer and retrieved very easily. You will actually be excited about storage.

Keep your strings of lights tangle-free by storing them inside empty toilet paper rolls or paper towel rolls. Or wrap them around the outside of empty paper towel rolls after notching the ends of the rolls.

We have 12 filled boxes, four marked trash bags, and four oversized boxes that have 25A, 25B, etc. labels on them. As you can tell, Christmas is big in our home. But when December comes, it's a neat, easy process. I don't have boxes and bags all over the garage floor for the whole month. I take down what I need, when I need it. In August when I begin to prepare for our holiday seminars (which begin in mid-September), I can take those items down from the garage shelves and look through my tablecloths, napkins, and props and freshen up those things that need attention. I can add new items and ideas to the old, and it's as easy as pumpkin pie.

Garlands, wreaths, and candles should be stored separately from ornaments. That way, next year you can start your holiday decorating without sorting through boxes of tree decorations. Large items such as wreaths can be stored in plastic trash bags labeled as if they were boxes by stapling a 3" x 5" card to the bag.

---

*The shepherds returned, glorifying and praising God for all the things they had heard and seen, which were just as they had been told*—Luke 2:20 (NIV).

# Traditions

Whether you have had traditions in your past or not, you can begin to implement them in your home, making a rich heritage for you and your children that can be passed on from generation to generation. It's not too late to start now. It makes no difference whether you're a family or an individual—you can still create memories and establish traditions. It's our responsibility to create good family memories and traditions that can be handed down to our children and our children's children. Psalm 71:17-21 says:

> O God, Thou hast taught me from my youth; and I still declare Thy wondrous deeds. And even when I am old and gray, O God, do not forsake me, until I declare Thy strength to this generation, Thy power to all who are to come. For Thy righteousness, O God, reaches to the heavens, Thou who hast done great things; O God, who is like Thee? Thou, who hast shown me many troubles and distresses, wilt revive me again, and wilt bring me up again from the depths of the earth. Mayest Thou increase my greatness, and turn to comfort me.

Dr. James Dobson points out:

> The great value of traditions comes as they give a family a sense of identity, a belongingness. All of us desperately need to feel that we're not just a cluster of people living together in a house, but we're a family that's conscious of its uniqueness, its personality, character and heritage, and that our special relationships of love and companionship make us a unit with identity and personality.

1. *Cookie exchange*—This is a great idea! Who invented it? We're not really sure, but it was definitely a woman with a busy schedule

and truly a stroke of genius! Instead of spending a fortune on ingredients and lots of time making a variety of cookies for the holidays, you can make a large batch of your favorites and swap them for many different kinds.

One of the most fun times I had was at a cookie exchange one morning with our church women. We had hot apple cider and lots of fellowship (this could also be done in the evening or with husbands). I received an invitation that instructed me to bring seven dozen cookies plus my recipe written on a recipe card that would be displayed by my cookie plate.

Our hostess had a lovely table prepared with candles for displaying our cookies. She prepared the hot cider and provided extra recipe cards for those of us who wanted to record other recipes. We were each given a paper tote bag (or you could use a box or tray) for taking cookies home. The tote bags added an extra touch. They aren't expensive, and we felt like kids in a candy store as we filled our bags.

Each one of us then took an equal number of each kind of cookie. We had a great time and went home with enough variety to please our families—not to mention some great recipes.

2. *Christmas cards*—Our Christmas cards begin to arrive early in December. We read and enjoy them at the moment. I then tear off the return address and check it with my address book to keep it current. The card then goes into our Christmas-card basket that I decorate with a holiday bow, holly, or a poinsettia. Our basket begins to fill up, and it stays where it's visible to the family.

After Christmas, this is the one thing we don't store away in boxes—at least not yet. Beginning January 1, we take our card-filled basket to our meal table and, before or after our meal, each member of the family draws out a card. We read the card and who it is from and then offer a prayer for that person or family. This tradition can last well into the new year. Many times I will drop a note to the family saying, "Thank you for your

Christmas card. Our family read it today, March 6, and we prayed for you. Blessings from our home to yours!"

3. *Family movies, videos, slides*—It's so much fun to see those old family movies, slides, or photos. Today's family, however, can videotape, so set aside an evening to do just that. It's fun to see how everyone has changed.

4. *Communion*—Christmas Eve or after the Christmas Day festivities are over, gather your family together and take turns sharing the meaning of that Christmas. The Christmas story can be read, and then join in a family communion. A good ending might be to sing "Joy to the World."

5. *Being a witness*—Invite adult friends and/or children's friends to your home to share a December evening with dinner or dessert. Plan songs, games, and some pertinent Scripture, and let them observe your example of Christ's love and the atmosphere of love in your home. Your family can follow up with prayers for the guests during the holiday season and into the new year.

6. *Tree cutting*—In some parts of the United States, you can go to a tree farm and choose and cut your own tree. We do this every year. It's become a fun tradition. In our family we have two perfectionists: our son, Brad, and our son-in-law, Craig. We plan a time when they can go with us so we're sure to bring home the perfect tree! Some tree farms have picnic areas, small zoos, and even offer caroling and hayrides. After we have chosen the tree, we go for a picnic or simple dinner or perhaps come home to cookies and hot cider, or maybe chili or hot soup. This creates a memory and brings the family together. If no tree farms are available in your area, a tree lot will serve the same purpose. It is also fun to take a picture of your tree untrimmed and then one after it's trimmed. You may not trim your tree the day you purchase it. If not, keep it in a bucket of water or wet sand. Hose it down to wash off the dust and dirt. It will keep healthy until the time to bring it into the house for trimming.

7. *Gifts for your neighbors*—Set up a cookie baking day with your children, grandchildren, or Sunday school children so they can experience a day in the kitchen. Bake and decorate the cookies, divide them into equal shares, place the cookies on colorful paper plates, wrap them in clear cello paper, tie with ribbons, and go around the neighborhood distributing the cookies a day or two before Christmas. You can also teach the children about manners as you visit your neighbors. This is a great way to spend a little time with neighbors you don't always visit. Don't be surprised if you get some gifts in return.

8. *Feed the homeless*—Sign up through your church, Salvation Army, or YMCA. In the past, this has been an enjoyable undertaking for our church family. It's a great way to build a better appreciation for the many blessings our family has, and at the same time teaches us to help those who are less fortunate than we are.

9. *Toys for tots*—Many local and civic organizations provide an opportunity for individuals and families to donate toys for distribution to needy families on Christmas Eve. Charles Colson's Prison Ministries has a program called "Angel Tree" where you can choose the name of a prisoner's child who has stated his or her Christmas wish, and you can provide this needy child with a gift. This is a great program available throughout America.

10. *Adopt-a-family*—There are many opportunities where your family can adopt a family in need. Help them with holiday food and gifts—it's a great bridge-builder.

---

*On the eighth day, when it was time to circumcise him, he was named Jesus, the name the angel had given him before he had been conceived*—Luke 2:21 (NIV).

# Tree-Trimming Party

1. *Special food*—Make it simple: tamales, tacos, hamburgers, pizza, make-your-own Sloppy Joes, spaghetti, Mexican mountains (make-your-own tostadas), etc.

2. *Make tree ornaments*—Use the following: macramé, paper, popcorn, noodles, straw, pipe cleaners, starch, eggshells, paper plates, popsicle sticks, tinsel, aluminum pans, paint, wooden spools, clothespins, string, fabric, cookies, or cranberries. Another idea is to personalize ornaments with a photo or date.

3. *Special music*—As you trim the tree, have your favorite Christmas music playing. Make it soothing enough that you can still have good family conversation. Sing along if you like.

4. *Invite a friend*—Let your children invite friends over so they, too, can experience this fun evening. After many years, many of our children's friends still recall the special time they had trimming our tree with us. Today our invited friends are our grandchildren. They just love coming over to help us with our tree. They are very curious about our ornaments, and want to know where they came from.

5. *Give a dated ornament each year*—All through the year, be looking for that special ornament that reflects the interest or personality of a family member or close friend. We love to find an ornament that depicts a basketball player, or someone skiing down snowy slopes, Mother cooking in the kitchen, or Dad fishing. Be sure to put the year's date on the ornament. Many of our tree trimmings go back 15 to 20 years in time. When Brad and Jenny got married, we gave each of them their old tree ornaments. They had instant tree trimmings for their first Christmases.

This tree-trimming party has become one of our very favorite Christmas traditions.

## The Manger with Baby Jesus

This tradition is probably the sweetest and most meaningful of all. A good friend of ours, Janet Patton from northern California, provided us with a home-built manger, that includes straw and a baby Jesus wrapped in meshed cloth.

As you build a "worship center" on a table in plain view for the whole family, have the following poem written using calligraphy and framed. Place this next to the manger:

---

*With excitement we anticipate the special Christmas morn. Rejoicing daily that our Christ child soon will be born. We'll spread our love throughout our home by preparing a cozy bed. A bed of straw to place his tiny little head.*

*As each day passes throughout the month we'll add a piece of straw for special love we've spread to one another, special little gifts or deeds and fun surprises to each other.*

*What fun our family will enjoy as we spread our love around.*

*On Christmas morn with joy and glee, we'll celebrate the Christmas tree. But most of all rejoice with praise the birthday of our King!*

---

Everything is displayed except Baby Jesus—hide Him away, but be sure to remember where. Next to the empty manger is a pile of straw cut into six-inch pieces. Beginning the first week in December, we gather as a family and talk about the manger and straw. Every day each member of the family does a good deed on his or her own, such as sharing toys happily, helping teacher pass out papers, or taking out trash without being asked. Then everyone puts a piece of straw in the manger. This can be done at the end of each day. Make sure to talk about the happiness you have given to one another.

As the month continues, the straw in the manger grows, and soon a cozy bed of straw fills the manger. Still no Baby Jesus appears. On Christmas Eve, after all the children are nestled in their beds and asleep, Mom and Dad will find Baby Jesus and place Him in His rightful spot. Straw or no straw, Baby Jesus always appears. Some years the manger may not be real cozy, but we have found that December is the best month of all for good behavior. Watch the excitement as the children race on Christmas morning to see if Baby Jesus has arrived. They head straight for the manger even before looking under the tree. Why? Because during the month we have been focusing on the real meaning of Christmas: Jesus' birthday.

## Other Christmas Traditions

We had dinner with some friends one evening and, as we walked up to their front door, we saw a banner in the window which said, "Happy Birthday, Jesus." I really loved it! It takes commitment to do something like this. They also had a birthday party for Jesus with cake, candles, and singing. What a beautiful expression of love for the children to experience! Here are a few more ideas to go along with your party:

- ✦ Invite neighborhood children and let them be a part of this special birthday party.

- ✦ Brings gifts or food which can be given to a needy family.

- ✦ Make craft items with a cross or the sign of the fish on them, such as a stuffed fabric heart which can be used as a necklace. Let the children wear these gifts home.

- ✦ Make bread-dough hearts and personalize them with a paint pen. Or paint *love, joy, peace*, etc. on them and use them as tree ornaments at home.

- ✦ Older children and adults can share testimonies.

✦ Share memorable Christmases.

✦ Have communion with friends.

Our friends Bob and Yoli Brogger probably do the best job of making Christmas memories. Their goal is to glorify Jesus during the month of December. Here are a few of their Christ-centered ideas:

✦ Yoli made a promise candle out of an oatmeal container. She covered the box with red felt then with yellow felt cut a piece in the shape of a flame and glued it onto the top. It looks just like a candle. They fill the box with Scripture promises. Each day of December, every member of the family draws out a promise and reads it around the table or at bedtime.

✦ They purchased a Christ-centered Advent calendar (one with Scriptures). You can also make these yourself. Each evening after dinner or before bedtime, the family gathers together and opens the appropriate window and reads the Scripture for that day.

✦ The Brogger family also has an Advent candle. You can use a regular candle and pretend there are numbers written on the side (1 through 25).

Each day of December, light the candle for about five minutes or until it burns down to the next date. They call it their holiday worship time:

1. The candle is lit.

2. The day's Advent calendar door is opened.

3. A Scripture is picked from the promise candle and read.

4. The Baby Jesus manger can be talked about and pieces of straw added.

5. Close with a short prayer.

The candle is then blown out. By Christmas Eve the candle will have burned way down. This is a special event in the Brogger home, and as the children have grown older they have taken the leadership roles.

✦ From the moment their friends approach their front door, they want them to know that within their home they celebrate something special. Yoli has a grapevine wreath and, in the center of this beautiful wreath, she puts a small nativity scene. Each year Yoli makes a few changes of ribbon, pinecones, or holly, but she always leaves on the nativity scene. As people stand waiting at their door, they can't help but look upon what the real meaning of Christmas is.

✦ Christmas stockings are always a lot of fun and can be handmade or store-bought. Again, the Brogger family does a very creative thing. They hang up a "joy" stocking. During the month of December, each family member puts thoughts, prayers, and love notes in the "joy" stocking. Then on Christmas Eve or Christmas Day the notes are pulled out and read. (This would be a great idea to do year-round.)

Singles can start traditions, too. Why not have a party for unmarrieds and include a spiritual emphasis? Light an Advent candle for five minutes and have a little Advent worship time, or read Scripture on your own each day of the month leading up to the twenty-fifth.

---

### Seven Fun and Free Ways to Celebrate Christmas

Christmas doesn't have to be the season to spend lots of money! Here are ways for you and your kids to celebrate frugally:

1. *Carol at night to spread cheer throughout your neighborhood. Bring a thermos of hot cocoa to keep everyone warm.*

2. *Visit Santa. Instead of heading to the mall, where lines are apt to be long, visit him at a local small store, library, or firehouse.*

3. *Bake Christmas cookies for your child's class at school. If you're pressed for time, make the "slice and bake" variety and decorate them with ready-made frosting.*

4. *Make a wreath from greenery in your own backyard, and let the children decorate it.*

5. *Attend a Christmas pageant at your elementary school—and don't forget to take plenty of pictures.*

6. *Enjoy the holiday lights in your hometown on a nighttime walk. It's fun to see your neighbors' decorations*

7. *Go to a recital at a local church. Many choirs sing The Messiah and other seasonal music.*

Christmas will be as special or as ordinary as you make it. You can be the architect of memories your children will carry with them for years—memories that will not only strengthen family bonds, but will also deepen their spiritual ties.

One of the most exciting things about traditions is that we can include others in them, even if they're not Christians. People aren't offended if everything is done in love and with a soft and gentle spirit. The Word that is read and vocalized during the month of December is going into the heart. God is honoring all the prayers we have prayed over Christmas meals and Scriptures we have read over the years.

Love the Lord your God with all your heart and with all your soul and with all your strength. These commandments that I give you today are to be upon your hearts. Impress them on your children. Talk about them when you sit at home and when you walk along the road, when you lie down and when you get up—Deuteronomy 6:5-7 (NIV).

# Advent

Rich in Christian tradition and symbolism, the Advent wreath brings beauty, light, and truth to our holiday season. The word *advent* means "coming." In all 39 books of the Old Testament, there is an air of expectancy. Someone is coming! During the Advent season, we anticipate the coming celebration of the birth of our Savior. Using a wreath during Advent season, you can teach and observe much of the symbolism of Christmas.

Advent begins on the fourth Sunday before Christmas and ends on Christmas Eve. A red or purple candle, symbolizing royalty, is lit on each of these four Sundays, and is traditionally accompanied by Scripture reading. A white candle is lit on Christmas Eve, signifying Christ's arrival. The color white speaks of the purity of our Lord. With the lighting of this last candle, the circle is complete, just as we are complete in Christ.

The circle of the wreath reminds us that His kingdom will have no end (Luke 1:33) and that God Himself has no beginning and no end. He has always existed and always will!

The evergreen tell us that Jesus brings eternal life: "For God so loved the world that he gave his one and only Son, that whoever believes in him shall not perish but have eternal life" (John 3:16 NIV).

A white dove on the wreath reminds us that the Holy Spirit descended as a dove.

However plain or elaborate your wreath, remember that God's Word is true. He loves you and sent His only Son into the world that you might have life and have it abundantly (John 10:10)!

## Family Advent Worship Time

The Lord is my light and my salvation—whom shall I fear? (Psalm 27:1 NIV).

Many families have established the Advent wreath as a wonderful tradition during their Christmas season. Here are some guidelines you may want to use:

1. Make a wreath using straw, evergreens, ribbon, etc. and place four red candles and one white candle around it.

2. Fourth Sunday before Christmas—Light the first red candle. Share Isaiah 2:1-5; 11:1-9; 40:3-11 showing the coming of the Messiah.

3. Third Sunday before Christmas—Light the second red candle. Share Luke 1:26-56 and Isaiah 7:13,14 telling of the mother of Jesus.

4. Second Sunday before Christmas—Light the third red candle. Share Luke 2:8-20, telling about the shepherds and angels. Share Matthew 2:1-12, telling about the wise men.

5. Last Sunday before Christmas—Light the fourth red candle. Share Matthew 2:13-23, telling of the flight into Egypt.

6. On Christmas Eve—Light the white and last candle. You may enjoy reading the Christmas story found in Luke 1:26-38 and Luke 2:1-20. Let the candles continue to burn until bedtime.

7. Rejoice! It's the birthday of the King who says, "I am the light of the world" (John 8:12 NIV).

Involve the whole family and take turns lighting and blowing out the candles. We believe this celebration of Christmas is pleasing to the Lord. It has taught our children the meaning of Christmas and helps us all to remember His birth and feel His presence in our homes.

# Scripture Readings for the Advent Wreath

The prophecies concerning Christ in the Old Testament which are expressly cited in the New Testament number more than 300! Here are just a few to choose from to add substance to the lighting of your Advent candles.

| Prophecy | Fulfillment |
| --- | --- |
| Psalm 72:10 | Matthew 2:1-11 |
| Psalm 118:26 | Matthew 21:9 |
| Isaiah 7:14 | Matthew 1:18; Matthew 1:22,23 |
| Isaiah 9:6,7 | John 1:19-34 |
| Isaiah 25:8 | 1 Corinthians 15:54 |
| Isaiah 28:16 | Romans 9:33; 1 Peter 2:6 |
| Isaiah 35:4-6 | Matthew 11:4-6 |
| Isaiah 40:3-5 | Matthew 3:3; Mark 1:3; Luke 3:4-6 |
| Isaiah 53:3-6,9,12 | Luke 22:37; Acts 8:32,33; 1 Peter 2:22 |
| Jeremiah 23:5,6 | Romans 3:21,22 |
| Jeremiah 31:31-34 | Hebrews 8:8-12; 10:16,17 |
| Micah 5:2-5 | Matthew 2:5,6; John 7:42 |
| Zechariah 9:9 | Matthew 21:4,5; John 12:14,15 |
| Zechariah 12:10 | John 19:37 |
| Malachi 3:1 | Matthew 11:10; Mark 1:2; Luke 7:27 |
| Malachi 4:5,6 | Matthew 11:13,14; Matthew 17:10-13; Mark 9:11-13; Luke 1:16,17 |

Christ, the church's one foundation, is the cornerstone of our holidays, the centerpiece of our celebration. May the peace that comes from knowing Christ the Lord be yours as you celebrate a year filled with happy holidays.

# November: Week 1—Things to Do

| Activity | Done (x) |
|---|---|

1._____ □

2._____ □

3._____ □

4._____ □

5._____ □

6._____ □

7._____ □

8._____ □

9._____ □

11._____ □

12._____ □

13._____ □

14._____ □

15._____ □

# November: Week 2—Things to Do

Activity                                                          Done (x)

1._____ ☐

2._____ ☐

3._____ ☐

4._____ ☐

5._____ ☐

6._____ ☐

7._____ ☐

8._____ ☐

9._____ ☐

11._____ ☐

12._____ ☐

13._____ ☐

14._____ ☐

15._____ ☐

# November: Week 3—Things to Do

Activity                                                           Done (x)

1._____ ☐

2._____ ☐

3._____ ☐

4._____ ☐

5._____ ☐

6._____ ☐

7._____ ☐

8._____ ☐

9._____ ☐

11._____ ☐

12._____ ☐

13._____ ☐

14._____ ☐

15._____ ☐

# November: Week 4—Things to Do

Activity                                                    Done (x)

1._____ ☐

2._____ ☐

3._____ ☐

4._____ ☐

5._____ ☐

6._____ ☐

7._____ ☐

8._____ ☐

9._____ ☐

11._____ ☐

12._____ ☐

13._____ ☐

14._____ ☐

15._____ ☐

# December: Week 1—Things to Do

Activity                                                    Done (x)

1._____ ☐

2._____ ☐

3._____ ☐

4._____ ☐

5._____ ☐

6._____ ☐

7._____ ☐

8._____ ☐

9._____ ☐

11._____ ☐

12._____ ☐

13._____ ☐

14._____ ☐

15._____ ☐

# December: Week 2—Things to Do

Activity                                                     Done (x)

1._____ ☐

2._____ ☐

3._____ ☐

4._____ ☐

5._____ ☐

6._____ ☐

7._____ ☐

8._____ ☐

9._____ ☐

11._____ ☐

12._____ ☐

13._____ ☐

14._____ ☐

15._____ ☐

# December: Week 3—Things to Do

Activity                                                    Done (x)

1._____  ☐

2._____  ☐

3._____  ☐

4._____  ☐

5._____  ☐

6._____  ☐

7._____  ☐

8._____  ☐

9._____  ☐

11._____  ☐

12._____  ☐

13._____  ☐

14._____  ☐

15._____  ☐

# December: Week 4—Things to Do

Activity                                                    Done (x)

1._____ ☐

2._____ ☐

3._____ ☐

4._____ ☐

5._____ ☐

6._____ ☐

7._____ ☐

8._____ ☐

9._____ ☐

11._____ ☐

12._____ ☐

13._____ ☐

14._____ ☐

15._____ ☐

# ✎Christmas Card Record✎

| Name | Address | Year | Sent | Rec'd |
|------|---------|------|------|-------|
| | | | | |
| | | | | |
| | | | | |
| | | | | |
| | | | | |
| | | | | |
| | | | | |
| | | | | |
| | | | | |
| | | | | |
| | | | | |
| | | | | |
| | | | | |
| | | | | |
| | | | | |
| | | | | |
| | | | | |
| | | | | |
| | | | | |
| | | | | |
| | | | | |
| | | | | |
| | | | | |
| | | | | |
| | | | | |
| | | | | |

# ∽Gifts Given ∾

| Occasion | To | Gift | Year |
|----------|-----|------|------|
|          |     |      |      |
|          |     |      |      |
|          |     |      |      |
|          |     |      |      |
|          |     |      |      |
|          |     |      |      |
|          |     |      |      |
|          |     |      |      |
|          |     |      |      |
|          |     |      |      |
|          |     |      |      |
|          |     |      |      |
|          |     |      |      |
|          |     |      |      |
|          |     |      |      |
|          |     |      |      |
|          |     |      |      |
|          |     |      |      |
|          |     |      |      |
|          |     |      |      |
|          |     |      |      |
|          |     |      |      |
|          |     |      |      |
|          |     |      |      |
|          |     |      |      |
|          |     |      |      |
|          |     |      |      |

# ∽Gifts Received∼

| Gift | Occasion | To | From | Thank You |
|------|----------|-----|------|-----------|
|  |  |  |  |  |
|  |  |  |  |  |
|  |  |  |  |  |
|  |  |  |  |  |
|  |  |  |  |  |
|  |  |  |  |  |
|  |  |  |  |  |
|  |  |  |  |  |
|  |  |  |  |  |
|  |  |  |  |  |
|  |  |  |  |  |
|  |  |  |  |  |
|  |  |  |  |  |
|  |  |  |  |  |
|  |  |  |  |  |
|  |  |  |  |  |
|  |  |  |  |  |
|  |  |  |  |  |
|  |  |  |  |  |
|  |  |  |  |  |
|  |  |  |  |  |
|  |  |  |  |  |
|  |  |  |  |  |
|  |  |  |  |  |
|  |  |  |  |  |
|  |  |  |  |  |
|  |  |  |  |  |
|  |  |  |  |  |
|  |  |  |  |  |
|  |  |  |  |  |
|  |  |  |  |  |

# ∽Shopping List∾

| Name | Gift/ Alternate | Size | Store | Cost Budget | Actual |
|------|-----------------|------|-------|-------------|--------|
|      |                 |      |       |             |        |
|      |                 |      |       |             |        |
|      |                 |      |       |             |        |
|      |                 |      |       |             |        |
|      |                 |      |       |             |        |
|      |                 |      |       |             |        |
|      |                 |      |       |             |        |
|      |                 |      |       |             |        |
|      |                 |      |       |             |        |
|      |                 |      |       |             |        |
|      |                 |      |       |             |        |
|      |                 |      |       |             |        |
|      |                 |      |       |             |        |
|      |                 |      |       |             |        |
|      |                 |      |       |             |        |
|      |                 |      |       |             |        |
|      |                 |      |       |             |        |
|      |                 |      |       |             |        |
|      |                 |      |       |             |        |
|      |                 |      |       |             |        |
|      |                 |      |       |             |        |
|      |                 |      |       |             |        |
|      |                 |      |       |             |        |
|      |                 |      |       |             |        |
|      |                 |      |       |             |        |
|      |                 |      |       |             |        |
|      |                 |      |       |             |        |
|      |                 |      |       |             |        |

# ⌒ Hospitality Sheet ⌒

Date: _____ Place: _____
Time: _____ Number of Guests: _____
Event: _____ Theme: _____

| Things to Do | ✔ | Menu | Preparation Time |
|---|---|---|---|
| One Week Before: | | Appetizers: | |
| | | | |
| | | | |
| Three Days Before: | | Entree: | |
| | | | |
| | | | |
| One Day Before: | | Side Dishes: | |
| | | | |
| | | | |
| Day Of: | | Salad: | |
| | | | |
| | | | |
| | | Dessert: | |
| | | | |
| | | | |
| Last Minute: | | Drinks: | |
| | | | |
| | | | |
| | | | |

| Guest List | RSVP Yes  No | Notes | Supplies |
|---|---|---|---|
| | | | Tables/Chairs |
| | | | Dishes |
| | | | Silver |
| | | | Glasses |
| | | | Centerpiece |
| | | | |
| | | | |

# Notes

## Chapter 4—Easter

1. Emilie Barnes and Sue Gregg, *Holiday Menus for Busy Women* (Riverside, CA: Eating Better Cookbooks, 1993), pp. 53-60.
2. Gloria Gaither and Shirley Dobson, *Let's Make a Memory* (Waco, TX: Word Books, 1983), pp. 28-34.
3. Marita Littauer, *Homemade Memories; Making Memories that Matter* (Eugene, OR: Harvest House Publishers, 1991), pp. 238-46 (adapted material).
4. Ibid., p. 246.

## Chapter 5—Mother's Day

1. Brenda Hunter, "The Value of Motherhood," *Focus on the Family*, 1986, pp. 9-12.
2. Gloria Gaither and Shirley Dobson, *Let's Make a Memory* (Waco, TX: Word Books, 1983), pp. 158-59.
3. Marita Littauer, *Homemade Memories; Making Memories that Matter* (Eugene, OR: Harvest House Publishers, 1991), pp. 248-51.
4. Emily Barnes and Sue Gregg, *Holiday Menus for Busy Women* (Riverside, CA: Eating Better Cookbooks, 1991), pp. 56-57.
5. Littauer, *Homemade Memories*, pp. 252-57.

## Chapter 6—Father's Day

1. Paula Yates Sugg, "In Memorial," *The Dallas Morning News* (September 26, 1993).
2. Bob Phillips, *Awesome Good Clean Jokes for Kids* (Eugene, OR: Harvest House Publishers, 1992), pp. 120-21.
3. Emilie Barnes and Sue Gregg, *Eating Better Cookbook* series (Riverside, CA: 1991). Taken from our various self-published cookbooks. Write to address on page 285.

## Chapter 7—Independence Day

1. "Very Innovative Parties," Women's Auxiliary to the Alumni Association, School of Dentistry, Loma Linda University, Loma Linda, CA, 1987. You may order it directly from: Very Innovative Parties, Loma Linda University, Dental Auxiliary, P.O. Box 382, Loma Linda, CA 92354.

**Chapter 8-Thanksgiving**

1. David Briggs, Associated Press, "Mealtime Blessings Give Thought to Food," *The Press-Enterprise*, Nov. 19, 1994, H-3.
2. From a tract published by Good News Publishers, Wheaton, IL.

**Chapter 10—Christmas**

1. Emilie Barnes and Sue Gregg, *Holiday Menus* (Riverside, CA: Eating Better Cookbooks, 1989), pp. 24-39.

For more information regarding speaking engagements and additional material, please send a self-adddresseed stamped envelope to:

**More Hours in My Day**
2838 Rumsey Drive
Riverside, CA 92506